God's Blueprint

=for=

Living

New Perspectives on the
Ten Commandments

God's Blueprint

==for==

Living

New Perspectives on the Ten Commandments

David A. Seamands

BRISTOL
BOOKS
WILMORE, KY 40390

Contents

Introduction

What exactly are the Ten Commandments? One common answer is, "The Ten Commandments are God's laws for today's lawless world." The key words in this phrase are "God" and "today," for the issue is whether the Ten Commandments really are God's law and, if they are, whether they still apply to modern life. In other words, are the Ten Commandments still absolute or are they obsolete?

Many people approach today's complex moral decisions like the scientist who received a large shipment of the latest books in his field. To his dismay he discovered he had no room for the new books on his library shelves, so he ordered his assistant to place every book more than 10 years old in storage. A lot of people today store away the Ten Commandments, considering them simply a matter of historical interest. Like a president emeritus the Ten Commandments have some sentimental value but no real authority.

Others think the Ten Commandments are not particularly useful for Christians, since "we are not under law but under grace." And some people simply don't like the Ten Commandments for obvious reasons—they enjoy breaking them.

A waitress in Atlantic City, who had served all kinds of people in that convention town, had never seen any group like the one attending a national convention for Methodist women some years ago. These women were teetotalers, so the waitress was not collecting the large tips she usually earned for serving liquor. When the

convention was over she observed with disgust, "These
Methodist women came here with the Ten Commandments and a 10 dollar bill, and they haven't broken
either." Now waitresses may be fooled, but as Christians we know better. Many of us should take a new look
at the old commandments.

But as we study the Ten Commandments, we will
not merely analyze these ancient guidelines as they appear in their original form in the Old Testament. After
all, we are not Jews but Christians. Our final word
comes from the New Testament. Therefore we must
look carefully at the way Jesus Christ and the New
Testament writers restate and often expand the original commandments.

Frankly, with the effects of sin being so obvious in
our world today, I don't think I need to sell you on the
importance of this subject. As we sift through the
Bible's moral guidelines, we'll discover that God—who
knows us better than we know ourselves—has given us
a remarkable plan for joyous living.

1

The Greatest Commandment Of All

One of them, an expert in the law, tested him with this question: "Teacher, which is the greatest commandment in the Law?"

Jesus replied: " 'Love the Lord your God with all your heart and with all your soul and with all your mind.' This is the first and greatest commandment. And the second is like it: 'Love your neighbor as yourself.' All the law and the prophets hang on these two commandments" (Matthew 22:35-40).

Interestingly, it was a lawyer who quizzed Jesus about the law. Lawyers spend much of their time asking questions in order to test people—that's their job. And that was the job of the New Testament scribes, the Jewish religious lawyers of their time.

By Jesus' day the Jews had 611 different commandments: 365 negative ones and 246 positive ones. A religious life had become a terrible burden to the sincere person who really wanted to please God. Competent lawyers were needed to keep track of all the commandments and to interpret them properly. So the question Jesus was asked was not really a trick question. Determining the greatest commandment was an issue that generated a great deal of controversy and debate in that day. It was inevitable that one day someone would ask the great Rabbi and Master Teacher, our Lord, for his opinion on this subject.

Actually, Jesus' answer did not introduce a radical new concept. Deuteronomy 6:5 contains the original command to "love God with all your heart...," and Leviticus 19:18 says "love your neighbor as yourself." Some modern Jewish commentators say that Jesus really didn't teach anything new; he was simply another rabbi who restated ancient laws.

New Neighbor

But Jesus did make this teaching totally new in several ways. First, he gave us a new image of God, one the world had not seen before. Second, he gave us a new definition of "neighbor." Jesus taught that your neighbor is not just a person of your own kind, your own kith and kin, to which Leviticus refers, or just those who have been neighborly to you. Instead Jesus explained that everyone who needs your help is your neighbor. Third, Jesus also revitalized this teaching by linking the two commandments together. In Luke's version of the story the lawyer quotes the commandments together, but Jesus is the one who says the second one is "like the first" or an extension of the first.

Above all, Jesus made the teaching totally new by perfectly demonstrating both commandments in his own obedient human life and his sacrificial death. He actually gives us the power to meet the otherwise impossible demands of the commands, especially through his gracious provision for the empowering presence of the Holy Spirit. This was something completely new.

But let's examine these two key commandments in detail. Think about the command, "Love the Lord your God with all your heart" for a moment. Immediately we discover one very serious problem. How in the world can

God command love? Doesn't that violate the voluntary nature of love? It's almost ridiculous. When we try to command love on a purely human level we find that we can hardly suggest it, let alone command it.

For example, do you know one of those helpful persons who is just sure that Mary and John are meant for one another? They scheme behind the scenes to get Mary and John together, certain that the two will fall in love. Only rarely does such maneuvering succeed. As a parent I long ago stopped suggesting potential sweethearts to my children. In fact, when my wife, Helen, and I mentioned someone, that person immediately became doubly obnoxious to our offspring.

The Heart Or The Will?

Love by its very nature is freely chosen, a voluntary giving of oneself to another. On the other hand when Jesus says, "you ought to love God, you ought to love your neighbor, you ought to love yourself," it sounds like a direct appeal to our will. This is a very serious dilemma. Love, we know, comes from the heart. We can command our will, but we certainly cannot command our heart.

To understand this baffling commandment, we must remember that the Scriptures give us promises as well as rules. Our Lord says things that are impossible for us are possible with God (see Matthew 19:26). Paul asserts in 1 Thessalonians 5:24, "The one who calls you is faithful and he will do it."

The gospel is not just good advice. The good news is that God does for us and in us what we could never do for ourselves. The Bible is full of impossible commands. But that's the point of having a divine Redeemer and Savior. He asks for more than we can give and then furnishes the difference himself. It's a free gift for the asking.

Augustine explains this as well as anyone in his profound prayer, "O Lord, give what thou commandst and then command what thou wilt." We are commanded to love. This is not an impossible request because God offers us the very love which makes obedience possible.

Many Loves

We should also note that the love God calls for is centered in the will and not in the emotions. This is *agape* love, one of the many Greek words for love. Unlike the Greek used by New Testament writers, English uses the word love in many different contexts. I love chocolate ice cream. I love basketball. I love a good book. I love my wife and children. Under our word "love" we lump these and other good, healthy loves with the many kinds of sordid relationships that exist between people today. But *agape* love is far above mere sentiment, likes or dislikes or emotions. It is even beyond the most exhilarating spiritual experience. This *agape* love is a principle by which we can order our lives. It is first and foremost not an emotion but a quality of the will, a commitment of the total person, an arranging of our lives' priorities. *Agape* love can be demonstrated but not defined. God so *loved* that he gave (see John 3:16).

Agape love does include our emotions, but it is just as real when we do not have conscious thoughts of fellowship. A person who has *agape* love is directed toward, surrendered to and living for God. So biblically speaking, love is more closely related to the will than to the emotions.

According to the Scriptures God alone is the source of *agape* love. Other loves, reflected in other Greek words, are natural to humanity, and there is nothing wrong with them. They are healthy, good forms of love. *Eros* love is physical love, sexual love, love for the beautiful and loving and intense patriotism for one's country.

Storge love is family affection, love for children and kin. Often translated in the Scriptures as brotherly affection, *philio* love includes warm personal friendship and the deep affection between husband and wife or between two friends. For example, Jesus and his beloved disciples exhibited *philio* love.

Agape Love

But *agape* love belongs only to God. It is not natural to humanity apart from God. So the real question boils down to this: how can I get this kind of *agape* love in my heart? Do I grit my teeth? Do I tell myself, "I *will* love God, I *will* love that person, I will love them, even if it *kills* me"? If this is my attitude, it probably *will* kill me. It will certainly kill *agape* love.

The Bible teaches that *agape* love does not begin with love at all. It begins with God. It begins with his love and my faith. "This is love," says John in 1 John 4:10, "not that we loved God, but that he loved us and sent his Son as an atoning sacrifice for our sins." 1 John 4:19 says, "We love because he first loved us." *Agape* love comes into our hearts as a response to God's *agape* love for us. Only love can beget love, only *agape* from God can reproduce it in our hearts. Love comes when we believe that we are loved and forgiven. Love comes when we accept the fact that we are accepted.

This is difficult for us to believe. All the laws that we have broken rise up within us and say, "It cannot be true. I cannot be loved because I am so unlovely. I cannot be accepted because I am unacceptable." This voice would be right if we were talking about *eros* or *storge* or *philio* love. These are "if" loves, "provided you do this" loves or "because you are this" loves. We humans often put strings on our love, and our reciprocating kind of love is not *agape*. Paul says, "God demonstrates his own [*agape*] love for us in this: While we were still sinners [while we were yet unlovely, unlovable, unacceptable, rebellious and hateful towards him] Christ died for us" (Romans 5:8).

It Begins At The Cross

One of my favorite Scripture verses is, "God was reconciling the world to himself in Christ [and here is the punch line] not counting men's sins against them" (2 Corinthians 5:19).

Agape love begins at the cross. That's the only possible place it can begin. When we look at the cross we see something unlike anything else in all the world. We see that at the very place we hurt God the most, where we must have looked the worst to God, that's the place where God loved us the most. Isn't that a miracle? Isn't that wonderful?

But is *agape* love some kind of "Operation Boot Strap" in which we whip up our own highest and best human love by meditating on the cross? No. Paul answers this question in Romans 5:5. Here the command to love God becomes a promise: "And hope does not disappoint us, because God has poured out his love into our hearts by the Holy Spirit, whom he has given us." God's *agape* love is poured into our hearts, not by our earnest efforts but by the Holy Spirit whom he gives unto us. God commands us to love him because he will, through his Holy Spirit, put his love in our hearts so that we *can* love him. Love begins with repentance and faith. It matures as we surrender to the Holy Spirit.

It may sound foolish, but a lot of people misunderstand this concept of surrendering to God. They ask, "If the Bible says to love God with all of my heart and mind and being, how can I do this and have time for anything else?" Indeed, some people feel that to fulfill the commandment they must leave all life's distractions and become hermits or ascetics who separate themselves from the secular, everyday world. Others think the commandment means they *must* enter full-time Christian service. Even people who haven't embraced either of these misconceptions may have a sneaking suspicion that they really can't please God and fulfill this command because of their station in life or profession.

But these ways of thinking are based on an error: the idea that the only way to love God is to always be thinking about God.

To illustrate, if you ask me, "Do you really love your wife?" I'd say, "Yes, I really love her."

"With all your heart?"

"I certainly do."

"Yes, but I saw you out in the yard concentrating on clipping the shrubs. I also saw you at a football game where you seemed to be engrossed in what you were doing."

I'd reply, "Wait a minute. That's ridiculous! Do you think my love for my wife vanishes when I concentrate on something else?"

Lord Of Personal Relationships

Remember that Jesus linked the two greatest commandments. We are not only told to love God, but we are also commanded to "love your neighbor as yourself." This destroys our compartmentalization of life into sacred and secular activities. Loving God, loving people, loving myself in the right way—they become one. He is the Lord of creation, the Lord of life and all personal relationships.

I don't want the mechanic who is repairing the jet I'm going to fly in to do a poor job because he's in a hurry to get to prayer meeting. Likewise, I don't want the surgeon who is operating on my child's heart to be thinking about anything else. Sometimes thinking about only God would be failing to love God supremely.

"Whatever you do, whether in word or deed, do it all in the name of the Lord Jesus, giving thanks to God the Father through him"(Colossians 3:17). Loving God is a full-time job, but it is accomplished in a thousand different ways as we love people and as we serve in the creation that God loved and said was good.

Living On The Level

To help us understand what role the greatest commandment plays in our lives, we should ask ourselves, "On what level of life do I live?" The lowest level is instinct, where we are driven by our desires and urges. The next level is law, mere outward obedience and conformity with no inward change. For people living at this level, religion is a duty and often a great drudgery. The third level might be a mixture of law and love, a life of duty with occasional flashes of devotion. People at this level are outwardly obedient but experience little enjoyment.

But thank God there is a higher, spirit-filled level, where love becomes the law of life. Duty becomes devotion and even joy. God enables us to love him and to delight in that love. He who commands us, who calls us to love him, is faithful. If we allow him, he'll move into our hearts and give us the power to live up to the greatest commandment of all.

2

Is Your God Fit To Love?

Jesus answered, "I am the way and the truth and the life. No one comes to the Father except through me. If you really knew me, you would know my Father as well. From now on, you do know him and have seen him."

Philip said, "Lord, show us the Father, that will be enough for us."

Jesus answered, "Don't you know me, Philip, even after I have been among you such a long time? Anyone who has seen me has seen the Father" (John 14:6-9).

Don't be shocked that we have yet to discuss even one of the original Ten Commandments. In this book we will focus not only on the actual commands in the Bible but also on the one who gave the commands. This is necessary because the commandments are based in the character of God: "I am the Lord your God, you shall do so and so or shall not do so and so." In the last chapter we discussed the command to love God, the greatest of all commandments. But is your God really fit to love?

God made us so that we trust good character and distrust bad character. God had to make us this way to keep us out of a lot of dangerous situations. A natural fear arises when we are suspicious about the character of a person or thing that we encounter. This keeps us from embracing lions and walking in front of trains. So if we believe God is untrustworthy, we will not be able to put our faith in him or love him.

I think this explains why many Christians have difficulty fully surrendering to God. We're made so that we just cannot surrender ourselves to a monster that we feel is cruel, vindictive, unreasonable or hateful. And deep down some of us, perhaps quite unconsciously, have these basic ideas about God. When we attempt to really surrender to him, these concepts may rise up to prevent us from completely trusting God, no matter how much our lips may say we surrender.

When I talk to people who are unbelievers, I often ask them to tell me their idea of God. Their responses often reveal hostility and resentment toward God. They don't like their kind of a god. Sometimes they even say that they are atheistic. And I always tell them that I don't believe in that kind of a god either, because that's not God. I rejected that caricature of God a long time ago. You see, these people are not really rejecting the living God but an utterly unworthy concept of God that has somehow been communicated to them.

We must all answer this question: Is my idea of God really big enough to love, or do I have an inadequate concept of God? You see, we are told to love God with our minds as well as our hearts. Since God created us so that we cannot love something or someone we do not respect, we have to have a God who is intellectually respectable.

God The Magician

Some of us, however, don't have that kind of God. For many of us God is a sort of magician with a wand. This god operates capriciously outside the laws of life. But as Einstein wrote over his laboratory at Princeton University: "God is a scientist, not a magician." Einstein had discovered in the laws of the universe a God he could respect, who is basically scientific. Of course

God is not a prisoner of the laws of the world he created. But we must have a God who is big enough to respect and a God who is big enough to worship with our minds.

Canon Raven says we should remember that all the facts are God's facts. Every single truth in psychology, sociology, geography, history or any field of knowledge is true to God. All truths can be integrated with the biblical idea of God. It was Jesus, not the devil, who said, "Then you will know the truth, and the truth will set you free" (John 8:32). Is your idea of God big enough to be intellectually respectable, to answer the problems of our world?

Besides being too small, our image of God may also be unloving. Is your god too mean or vindictive to love? Is he too demanding? Some of our amazingly distorted concepts of God are astounding. John Wesley once told some of his opponents, "Your God is my devil." In other words, they were attributing moral characteristics to God that Wesley ascribed to the devil.

Too-Small God

I doubt if we could ever improve on J.B. Phillips' little book, *Your God is too Small.* If you have never read it, I advise you to do so. In the first part of the book Phillips lists many of the common varieties of unchristian ideas of God. He notes that these concepts are so utterly unworthy and so childish that they cannot endure the storms of life for five minutes.

Phillips assigns some clever names to these common misconceptions. For example, the idea of God as "resident policeman" occurs when we make conscience our god. People who have super-sensitive and very morbid consciences often falsely regard the nagging inner frustration of conscience as the voice of God. Phillips calls another misconception the "parental hangover." This is the god that we form out of the relics of our childhood training. We take all the scraps of truth we learned here and there, throw them all together and distort them. This results in an unfit kind of parent-child relationship which we use as our model for God.

A college sophomore once wrote me the following letter:

"I have a wonderful Christian mother, but she lives in fear and trembling of the God of Israel. And she was always so strict with me that I live in fear of him too. Surely no one would ever say that my mother is not a really consecrated woman. But the God she taught me to revere doesn't sound like the God you preach about. Mother says I shouldn't be filling my mind with those strange ideas. I try so hard not to do anything that would displease God, but now that I am in college away from mother, I am more and more nervous for fear that I don't really know how to be sure that I am not displeasing to the Lord."

This young man was following his mother's God. Actually, it might be more accurate to say that he was following his mother and had confused the voice of God and the voice of Mamma. Sometimes it's difficult to sort these things out in our lives. Even adults can carry spiritual scars from unworthy concepts of God that result from faulty training in the home, Christian and otherwise.

"Try Harder"

Another unworthy picture of God Phillips identifies is "perennial grievance." This kind of god is always saying, "That's not quite good enough. You've got to do better than that if you are to please me and if I am to love you." This god is not merely perfect and holy, but he is a perfectionist who can never accept anything except perfect performance. If this is the god you worship, you are probably having difficulty loving your god. This kind of god is an increasingly demanding tyrant who asks for more and more and always says, "Try harder." This god drives some of us to spiritual and nervous breakdown. Because this kind of god keeps us constantly filled with anxiety and guilt, down deep it's impossible to love him. You may serve him, respect him, be in awe of him and obey him, but it's unlikely that you truly love him. More likely, you resent him.

This wrong image of God represented is like the elder brother's view of his father in Luke 15. He's the brother who stayed home while his younger brother spent his inheritance in a far country. The older brother sweated it out, working in the fields. He obeyed every command. He was a good boy. But inside he felt a hard core of resentment for the old man. "Look, these many years I've served you and you never gave a feast for me," he says when his father invites him to celebrate his wayward brother's return. In spite of the loving father's pleading, the angry older son would not attend the party. Is that how you feel toward God? If so, you will find him too mean and hateful to really love.

But perhaps we're blaming other people too much for giving us wrong concepts of God. Things in our own lives can distort our spiritual outlook. We can have a kind of a spiritual astigmatism that distorts our image of God. In counseling people I've found that any god that comes out of the shadow of our hearts will not be the true God but a caricature of him. The Lord tells the wicked man in Psalm 50:21, "You thought I was altogether like you."

Creating God In Our Image
Some of us have created God in our own image and thus distorted him. We project unworthy, unlovable, hateful ideas from our minds onto the person of God. We do this for two main reasons.

First, our guilty fears are perhaps the greatest image perverter of all. I have talked to many people who say they just can't love God or believe in him, and it turns out that the reason is that they cannot accept God's forgiveness. They cannot believe that God forgives them and accepts them. They cannot believe in a God of love. Why? Because some hidden sin and guilt in their life gives them a sense of fear.

I've been amazed by the terrible pictures of God these people carry in their minds. They see God as a horrible monster, an omnipotent devil in the sky anxious to catch them, to punish them, to send them to hell. This caricature of God is the projection of their awful guilt and fear. They attribute their own self-loathing and the anger they feel about their own violated consciences to God.

Hiding From God

Adam and Eve did this. It is the first symptom of the disease of sin and was the first consequence of sin in the Garden of Eden. You remember that until a certain day, Adam and Eve had always eagerly awaited the cool of the evening when the Lord God would come down and have fellowship with them. It was the most beautiful part of their day. God was their friend. He walked and talked with them. All day long they'd wait expectedly, and when they'd finally hear God's footsteps they'd rush out to meet him with love and friendship. But this particular evening, after they had disobeyed God, they were hiding behind trees in the garden. They were ashamed. But God hadn't left them or forsaken them. God still came down in the cool of the evening to fellowship with them. God's footstep and voice were the same, but Adam and Eve heard them differently. Like them, when we sin God's footstep and voice seem different. Like Adam and Eve we too run and hide.

When we do something wrong we start hiding from our friends, from people, from God. We cannot believe in God's love because we hate ourselves and we assume that God also hates us. Sin leads to guilt and guilt to fear and fear to hate. This becomes a vicious circle. When we think God hates us, he becomes a hateful god in our eyes.

We humans tend to consider sins of the flesh, sexual sins, as "the big ones." Jesus, however, often treated them less seriously than heart-hardening sins of the spirit, such as pride and hypocrisy. But somehow when we do wrong things in this regard we often project our tremendous guilt and self-hatred onto the character of God.

Emphasis On Wrath

I'll never forget when, many years ago, we took a group of young people to Nashville to be interviewed by my denomination's missionary personnel committee, of which I was a member, for possible missionary service. One young lady who went with us had a particularly fervent desire to become a missionary. But as we studied the application forms that she sent our committee in advance, we all began to notice something. Her answers reflected an unhealthy over-emphasis upon God's wrath, judgment, punishment, sin and guilt. We talked to her about this, and she hedged around a good deal. Nevertheless, she was such a fine person and I knew her so well that I went to bat for her because of her talent.

After that first interview the committee asked her to talk to me. When we got back from Nashville she came to my office, and we talked. In tears she told of a sexual sin she had committed many years before. She felt condemned and that God just *had* to punish her. Her whole concept of God was colored by the lens through which she viewed him. I was glad we discussed this sin and could place it on the cross where all the garbage of our past belongs. She prayed and found great release.

She was eventually accepted by the mission board and performed some years of very acceptable service. Since our conversation she has written me several times about how, slowly but surely, she has begun to see God more clearly and to understand his love and power and forgiveness.

Unforgiving Spirit

A second perspective that discolors our picture of God is, I believe, any form of repressed resentment for other people. Often people are unable to receive God's forgiveness because they cannot forgive someone else. As time passes this tendency worsens, and they begin projecting their own resentments and unforgiving spirit onto the character of God. Soon they are resisting and rejecting not the true God but a misrepresentation of God.

Several years ago Dr. Tom Carruth and I were helping lead a spiritual retreat in a southern state. As the Bible teacher of that retreat I was giving a series on the Holy Spirit. One morning I spoke on the theme: "The Holy Spirit, the spirit of love."

After the morning service I went to the cafeteria where I waited in line to be seated at one of the tables. Suddenly I felt a very distinct, strong inner impression that I ought to sit at a certain table. Well, I looked over at the table which was full of rather young women and saw only one empty chair.

Naturally, I suspected my guidance in this regard. To determine whether it was the Holy Spirit or some other spirit, I lifted the situation up in a moment of prayer to the antiseptic guidance of the Holy Spirit. Still

I felt the same strong urge to sit at the table. So rather hesitantly I took my tray over there and sat down in the only empty chair.

A Spiritual Hammer
The moment I sat down, the lady next to me heaved an audible sigh. "Thank God," she said. "From the time you walked into the dining hall I have been praying that you'd sit here and talk to me." God had spoken to her through the morning message. Actually, he had spiritually hit her with a hammer. Later we met and she told me her story.

Her father had died when she was 13 years old. Overwhelmed by the loss and sorrow, her mother began drinking and soon became an alcoholic. Life in that home became an absolute hell for the next few years.

Since the young woman was very talented musically, she joined a nightclub and began playing in a jazz combo at the age of 18. While she was working one night, a disgusting older man had tried to seduce her. She didn't see that man again until over a year later when, to her absolute horror and shock, her mother married this very man. The young woman already hated her mother for her alcoholism, and now her hate intensified. She ran away from home, hating both her mother and her new stepfather deeply and bitterly.

Shortly after this she began to have all kinds of rashes, asthma, severe back pains and other disorders. She continued to have all these problems, even though by the time I talked with her she was married to a naval officer of considerable rank and had children. Her stepfather had recently left her mother, and her mother was all alone, a pitiful case. The daughter was trying to keep her still alcoholic mother away, but her mother insisted on visiting. The mother would try to pick up her grandchildren, but the daughter wouldn't allow it. She still hated her mother and taught her own little children to hate their grandmother. And since hatred for persons breeds a hatred for God, God increasingly became this young woman's angry, vengeful deity. She began to resent him.

Bad To Worse

She was an organist in a large Presbyterian church which she and her family attended. Nevertheless, things in her life were going from bad to worse. Because of her twisted concept of God, she found it increasingly difficult to really love her husband. It's impossible to resent God and resent some person and still be able to love.

As her own marriage became shaky her hate became all consuming. This is the story that she poured out to me at the retreat.

That night we again preached on the Holy Spirit, and this lady came to the altar. She said that all afternoon she had been trying to believe in God's love and forgiveness. God had made it plain to her that, if anything was to happen in her life, she'd have to surrender all her terrible resentment for her mother and stepfather and for God himself. But she said she just could not do it.

Dr. Tom Carruth and I called some friends and we laid hands upon her. She prayed, Dr. Tom prayed, we all prayed. And something happened in her heart, though it wasn't really obvious that night.

The next day she gave a radiant testimony about how something had happened in her heart while we were praying for her. She said it was as though a cancerous lump had been removed. Her hatred and resentment had left and she felt a great sense of forgiveness and peace and God's love flooding her soul.

Now, in cases like this where emotions have been

damaged for years I sometimes wonder, "Is it real? Is it going to last?" But several months later I received a letter from her. She wrote that she just had to share the wonderful blessings that had been hers since that night at the retreat. Her heart had overflowed with love and joy ever since. She'd called everybody and told her neighbors about her new birth. People had even told her she had a new sparkle in her eyes. She also said her asthma and back pains had vanished.

Honest Self-Evaluation

What can we do to change our wrong concepts of God?

First of all, we must face our ideas of God and evaluate your own lives honestly. We can't blame others. We must look squarely at ourselves.

I remember a woman who was troubled by the problem of evil. It was all she could talk about. "How can there be a God of love when there is so much evil in this world?" she'd ask. I talked with her and counseled her and suggested books. Finally I bought C.S. Lewis' great book on this subject, *The Problem of Pain*, and I gave it to her.

She kept it a long time. "Yes, yes, I'm going to read it," she'd say, but she never did read it. She never will read it. You see, the problem of evil is her red herring, her excuse. She doesn't dare risk letting Lewis or anyone else knock the props out from under her rationalizations. She wants to live her own selfish way and have a supposedly rational reason for blaming God for all the failures in her life.

Face yourself in all honesty. Look for the excuses. Where are you at fault for creating a wrong concept of God?

Better yet, don't just look at your own face in a mirror but look at the face of Jesus Christ. The only true

picture of God is in his face. "Anyone who has seen me
has seen the Father," Jesus tells us in John 14:9.
Methodist missionary E. Stanley Jones said, "You and I
know almost nothing about God except what we see in
Jesus Christ, and most of the little we do know is
wrong." Look to Jesus, study his life, see how he dealt
with people.

Near The Cross

And, above everything else, draw nearer to the cross.
Calvary contains nothing vindictive or negative or unhealthy. There God took our sins upon himself. Our
lives were cleansed and forgiven. Our only hope is to
look at the love in the face of Jesus Christ. Here is love
that is unconditional, complete, without limits; a love
that loves the unlovely, the unlovable, the unacceptable. Our God increases his love in the face of our
rejection and resistance. He even loves us when we're
committing the worst sin of all, namely, failing to
believe that he loves us. At the cross our concepts of God
are cleansed, and we find a God to whom we can surrender ourselves unreservedly, unconditionally. If our
God is the God who comes to us in Jesus Christ, he is a
God we can give ourselves to totally.

3

Let God Be God

I am the Lord your God, who brought you out of Egypt, out of the land of slavery. You shall have no other gods before me (Exodus 20:2-3).

For even if there are so-called gods, whether in heaven or on earth (as indeed there are many "gods" and many "lords"), yet for us there is but one God, the Father, from whom all things came and for whom we live; and there is but one Lord, Jesus Christ, through whom all things came and through whom we live (1 Corinthians 8:5-6).

Too many people just sort of reach into the Bible and grab the Ten Commandments out of thin air. Sometimes when they do so they get not only thin air but a lot of hot air too.

I say this because when we discuss the Ten Commandments with unbelievers, those outside the faith, we hear a lot of phrases like "outmoded rules," "outdated laws" or "ancient codes." People in the faith, Christians, also criticize the commandments. When someone just plucks the commandments out of the Bible we often hear the word "legalism."

As we discussed in the last chapter, the Ten Commandments do not begin with the prohibitions—the "you shall nots." The Ten Commandments begin with the character of God. God tells us who he is before he gives us a single rule: "I am the Lord your God, who brought you out of bondage." Therefore, this first great commandment to have no other gods is rooted in two great facts: the character of God and his covenant relationship with the people to whom he is issuing his commandments.

You almost have to start at the beginning of biblical history to fully understand who God is and how he relates to his people. God called Abraham out of the paganism, polytheism and idolatry of the cultures around him to worship and obey the one true God.

Abraham was perhaps the greatest man of faith who ever lived. Without any external resources such as the Bible or churches, Abraham went out from his homeland literally not knowing where he was going and really knowing little about the God who was guiding him.

Jacob, who lived almost 300 years before the Ten Commandments were given, also vowed to serve the one true God (Genesis 35:2,3). He commanded everyone—children, his entire household—to "Get rid of the foreign gods you have with you, and purify yourselves and change your clothes. Then come, let us go up to Bethel, where I will build an altar to God. . . ."

Context For The Commandments
But to really understand the Ten Commandments, and particularly this first commandment, we must consider them in the context of the great incidents that took place just before they were given: When God had delivered his people out of slavery in Egypt in dramatic fashion (see Exodus 5-14).

Now, many Bible scholars point out that the 10 plagues God sent to Egypt to convince Pharaoh to let the Israelites leave corresponded to certain Egyptian gods. These included gods of the air, gods of light and darkness, gods who were supposed to protect cattle and gods of the Nile River. The 10 plagues showed the Egyptians that their gods were myths, powerless before the

true and living God. Not only did the Egyptians need
this graphic demonstration, but the children of Israel,
God's own people, did too. Unfortunately, like all of us
who are surrounded by idolatry, the chosen people had
become attracted to the popular local gods of Egypt. God
wanted the children of Israel to know that he is not just
the chairman of the board of gods; he is the *only* God.

Therefore, when giving the Ten Commandments
God first establishes who he is: "I am the Lord your God,
who brought you out of Egypt, out of the land of slavery."
God then establishes his place in our lives. For if he is
who he says he is, that means he has a right to demand
worship and unqualified allegiance and love.

Salvation And Deliverance

This is a pattern used throughout the Bible. Almost
every Scripture passage that contains laws or ethical
guidelines is preceded by vast sections on the doctrine
of salvation and deliverance. The book of Romans is a
classic example. The first 11 chapters of Romans tell the
whole magnificent plan of salvation. It is as though God
is saying, "I am the Lord your God who brought you out
of bondage, who through Christ has forgiven your sins
and delivered you and cleansed you." After these chapters, the twelfth chapter begins: "Therefore, I urge you.
. . ." Why are we being urged? Because of the kind of
God we have, and what he has done for us. Then follow
almost four chapters of ethical rules and principles of
conduct. We might call them modern Christian commandments. Because God can say, "I am the Lord your
God, who delivered you out of bondage," he has a claim
on us.

You see, understanding who God is and what God
has done is essential to comprehending the Ten Commandments. That's why we spent so much time discus-
sing wrong concepts of God in the last chapter.

But even if we have an accurate concept of God, we may not grasp the meaning of the commandments. Some moderns criticize the Bible's commandments for not being really up-to-date. They say the first commandment should not be "you shall have no other gods before me," but, in this age of atheism and unbelief, "you shall have at least one god." Our modern danger, some say, is not in having too many gods but in having no gods.

At Least One God?

And yet this criticism points to the genius of the first commandment and one of the many proofs of its divine origin. It wisely avoids the foolish and futile assertion that there is but one God. God knows our hearts better than we do. He knows that every person has some kind of a god in his or her life. God knows that anything, however worthy or unworthy, to which an individual gives his or her ultimate devotion, service and energy is the god of that person's life. God knows that every human being is incurably religious and will worship some kind of a god or something beyond herself or himself. History and anthropology confirm that most people, however primitive or advanced, worship.

The decision before us is not between atheism or God. It is not the issue of God or no God. That is not our choice. The question is which god we will worship—the true and the living God who came to us in Jesus Christ or a substitute god? Inevitably we must look to something beyond ourselves. This "something" helps us make choices in life. It gives us a set of values or priorities that serve as a reference point. It becomes the determining factor in our lives so that gradually and perhaps imperceptibly we become like the god we worship.

Every god stamps his worshiper with his trademark.

Your god is leaving his mark upon your life. Martin
Luther said it beautifully: "Whatever then the heart
clings to, whatever thy heart relies upon, that is properly thy god."

We must let God be God, the true and living God.
That's why the Bible so fiercely opposes every form of
idolatry. The greatest sin described in the Scriptures is
not the breaking of commandments but idolatry.
Idolatry is misplaced allegiance, making a commitment, having a love, a priority, a god which displaces
and dethrones the true and living God.

Cycle Of Worship

The history of the people of Israel is almost mono-
tonous with its cycle of worshiping the true God, then
gradually turning back to the false gods and the idols.
But isn't that the story of our own lives? That's why the
New Testament is filled with admonitions to be careful
of idols. Paul sums this up when he says, "You are slaves
to the one whom you obey" (Romans 6:16).

Many people however, think we have overcome our
attraction to idols. They say, "I agree that primitive
humanity had to worship something, but modern man
has outgrown that. We neither need a god nor do we
have gods." But how wrong we are when we think this.
The truth is, while we no longer have a whole Sears catalog of gods like the people of ancient Greece and Rome,
we moderns are essentially the same. We may have
eliminated the catalog, but we still have the merchan-
dise. The old gods never die; they don't even fade away.
They just change their masks and return with new and
improved techniques for deceiving us, seducing us and
destroying us.

The earlier people were perhaps better off than we
are today because they were more honest about it. The
ancients personified the functions of life, making gods

out of all sorts of things. They had Mars, the god of war; Eros, the god of pleasure; Venus, the goddess of beauty; Cupid, the god of love; Narcissus, the god of self-glorification; Bacchus, the god of liquor and so forth. We may laugh at this, but at least people never forgot that they had to choose from a vast number of gods who were constantly competing for allegiance and devotion.

We haven't eliminated these false gods by getting modern and smart. The gods are still with us, and they not only make us in their own image, but they also destroy us.

So you see, the commandments that we find in Exodus *are* true to life. It is psychologically and spiritually true that our morals depend upon the character of our God. Our choice is not between the true God and no god but between the true God and some lesser god, some unworthy object which would claim our devotion and our service and become the god of our lives.

Today's Surrogate Gods

The tragedy today is that so many of us, like people in the book of Kings, claim to serve the Lord but really serve other gods. Modern man has shaped a pantheon of false gods. They're so subtle, so clever, so taken for granted as a part of everyday life that it is difficult to keep them off God's solitary throne in our hearts. You and I may laugh at the heathen bowing before a grotesque idol but be totally unaware that the sophisticated substitute that we have put in God's place is just as grotesque. Our god may be even more spiritually destructive than the idol in that Stone Age village.

Let's look briefly at some of the false gods that strive to usurp the place of the true God. These surrogate gods determine our practical everyday choices and our moral standards. Space prohibits enumerating all of the false gods abroad in our day. However, we can look at a few to illustrate that most of our idols result from taking some good gift that God has given us, misusing that gift and making it the god of our lives.

Venus, Baal and . . .

One of our most powerful modern gods is sex. This is not surprising. Humanity has always deified sex. In Old Testament times it was Baal worship. India has always had its fertility gods and goddesses. The Romans had their temples to Venus and others. But those gods were different from today's sex god. In a sense those cults deified sexuality, glorified it and made it a means of worshiping some particular god or goddess. This sex-related worship was something separate in a compartment of life. But today sex itself has become the god of many. It is the substitute for meaning and purpose. This great god Sex leers at us from advertisements and wiggles at us from TV screens. Most modern novels and movies are simply invitations to become Peeping Toms. Hail the great goddess Sex. Hollywood is its prophet, and the sordid stories of its stars are its sacred scriptures.

Oh, how pathetic, how pathological, how beautiful was Marilyn Monroe, dead now for more than a quarter of a century. You'd think we'd let her rest in peace, but she is still the subject of songs, articles and books. In my files I have an old clipping, a six-page spread from *Life* magazine on Marilyn Monroe in which she says some interesting things. She says she doesn't like being the sex symbol of the United States because a symbol becomes a thing and is no longer a person. This is a profound insight. But she says, "If I have to be a symbol of something I'd rather have it be sex than anything else." The clipping is dated August 3, 1962. The night of August 4, 1962 Marilyn Monroe ended her own life.

When we use one of God's precious gifts, like sex, as

God commands and do not abuse it by making it central in our lives, it will bring ecstasy and great joy. But when we take a gift from God, forget the Giver and live for it, it will eventually let us down. The abuse of any of God's gifts, by making it a substitute for God himself, ultimately destroys the gift and its capacity to bring the joy for which it was created and intended.

The Science God

For example, the great gift of our minds and our education are meant to be used to master the world and its environment, to learn truth and to conquer the enemies of life. But what has happened? Education has become an end in itself. Science has become a god. We've pinned our hopes on it for years. And now the very technology and education which was supposed to lift us to some kind of heaven by our own atomic bootstraps and make the world a paradise with food, shelter, heat and light for all has turned into a Frankenstein-like monster. Science threatens to destroy everything it has made, to reverse the prophecies of Isaiah and turn the blossoming rose back into a radioactive desert. All of our electronic knowledge and our scientific equipment only seems to bring us closer to an electronic jungle where big brother will be watching over us.

Astronaut Buzz Aldrin was the second man to step on the moon. I remember years ago seeing him interviewed on NBC's *Today* program. He told of the years of education, hard work, dreams and rigorous discipline he spent preparing for that day, including earning a Ph.D. in a very difficult, specialized subject. He was finally chosen to go with Neil Armstrong on that historic mission to the moon.

But during the interview Aldrin also told of his later emotional breakdown and slow, painful recovery. This crisis didn't have anything to do with the moon or with space travel or weightlessness. What caused it? Over and over again Buzz Aldrin kept saying that the breakdown resulted from the terrible disillusionment he felt after working so hard, achieving every goal set before him and then finding it all empty when it was over. He had taken a good thing and made a god out of it, and it did what all false gods do—it turned around and destroyed its worshiper. That's what inevitably happens when we turn God's gifts into substitute gods.

A Real Religious Drama

A favorite story of mine illustrates this truth. Many years ago Dr. Harold Ehrensperger, a great pioneer in the field of Christian drama, decided to see the famous Passion play in Oberammergau, Germany, to get the feel for religious drama. While there he stayed with a fine Lutheran Christian family.

It is the custom to choose the actors for the Passion play from the local community. The play's directors study people and match them with the New Testament character whose life is most like their own. Sometimes actors study and train for years in order to play a particular part.

Now in the home where Dr. Ehrensperger was staying lived a young teenager named John. Deeply religious, John confided to Dr. Ehrensperger one day that his lifelong ambition was to grow up and actually become John in the Passion play. He said, "I don't think I'll ever be worthy to play the part of Jesus Christ, but if I work hard enough, if I discipline myself, if I learn to love as John loved, maybe I'll be chosen to be John the beloved disciple."

Dr. Ehrensperger and John became fast friends. They corresponded for several years after Dr. Ehrensperger returned to the United States. Then great changes came to Germany. Hitler came into power and the youth of the land began to follow the "new messiah." John's letters became fewer and fewer and finally stopped altogether.

For several years Dr. Ehrensperger didn't hear from John. Then came the war. Hitler moved across Europe, and his victories shook the world. One day an envelope came to Dr. Ehrensperger. It was postmarked Poland, October, 1939. He eagerly opened the envelope and was disappointed. It contained no letter, only a clipping from a German newspaper. On the front page was a large picture. In the center of the picture, smiling, flushed from his recent victories, stood the triumphant Adolf Hitler with his hand raised, surrounded by his officers.

Dr. Ehrensperger stared at the picture. It couldn't be. Yes, it was. There was no doubt about it. Next to Adolf Hitler himself, tall, fully grown, handsome, in the uniform of Hitler's own personal aide-de-camp, was John. Then Dr. Ehrensperger looked closely, and penned on that newspaper clipping was an arrow pointing to Adolf Hitler with the words written in English, "Jesus Christ" and another arrow pointing to John with the words, "John, his beloved disciple."

No Other Gods

Does it make a difference who the god of your life is? Yes indeed! It makes the difference between life and death. "I am the Lord, your God. You shall have no other gods before me."

Let God be God, the true God, the living God. We talked about false concepts of God in the last chapter because idolatry is not simply the worship of those things outside of ourselves that we create with our own hands. Idolatry is also those false and unworthy conceptions of God that we hold and worship. We saw how miserable and unhappy we as Christians can be when we have the wrong concept of God. Let *God* be God.

A second way to examine this truth about the first commandment is to put the emphasis the other way: Let God be *God*. The emphasis is on his character, as our Savior and Deliverer. As we've discussed, the commandments are based on God's character. Let God be *God* in our lives. This is important because some of us can have the right conception of God and yet crowd him into a lesser place in our hearts and lives. Paul says, "yet for us there is but one God" (1 Corinthians 8:6). For us that God is the God and Father of our Lord Jesus Christ.

The Singular Difference
Elton Trueblood pointed out that the number one is different from all the other numbers. It's different not only in degree but in kind. He says our languages have caught this deep insight. Singular means one and only one while plural means more than one. How many more? It really doesn't make any difference. It can be two or three or two or three million or ten billion. There is a greater difference between one and two than between two and two billion.

We can illustrate this in human terms. The man who has one wife is fundamentally different from the man who has two wives. Now the man who has two or three wives or the sheik who has 400 wives are all in the same category. They are totally different from the man who has one wife because he says, "I can only commit my affection to one. I cannot divide it. I cannot share it. I can love only one." We Christians have only one God. That's why gods is not the plural of the word God. That's why we spell it with a small g—God has no plural. He is one.

Jesus restates the first commandment in Matthew 6:24, "No one can serve two masters." Oh, but we can try, can't we? And many of us do. The result is inner division and destruction. Some of us have the right concept of God. But where do we put him? Not at the center of our lives.

Fragmentation And Neurosis

Just as we have a built-in desire to worship some god, we also have built into our personalities the need for only one God. We cannot love and serve more than one God. We cannot love God with just a fraction of ourselves. If we do, we become fragmented. Polytheism in my heart will produce polytheism in my personality and emotions. The Bible calls it idolatry. Psychiatry calls it neurosis. The whole point is that we are built for only one God. When we fragment our loyalties, our emotions and our lives become off center.

I'm not giving a simplistic answer to all of life's difficulties. But I think the basic cause of our problems, whatever they may be, is that God, the true God, the Father of our Lord Jesus Christ, is not God of our lives. Instead we have tried to assign him to a corner of our hearts. The tension in our lives occurs because we can't serve two masters.

So, who is your God? And where is your God? On the throne? Or do you have a divided loyalty? The first commandment is essentially saying, "I am the Lord your God. I am your Savior. Your Deliverer. You belong to me. I have rights over you. I am yours, you are mine. Therefore you shall have no other gods before me."

Some years ago in a Scottish town someone placed an unusual advertisement in the local newspaper. On the front page of the newspaper, a conspicuously placed notice asked the reader to look on the back page. When the reader turned to the back page, it was empty. But those who looked closely saw, in the lower right hand corner in small print, these words: "Is this where you are putting God?"

4

The God Who Tolerates No Rivals

You shall not make for yourself an idol in the form of anything in heaven above or on the earth beneath or in the waters below. You shall not bow down to them or worship them; for I, the Lord your God, am a jealous God, punishing the children for the sin of the fathers to the third and fourth generation of those who hate me, but showing love to a thousand generations of those who love me and keep my commandments (Exodus 20:4-6).

"Wait a minute," someone says. "I can understand what you have been saying, that the basis of the commandments is in the character of the one who gave them, the one who began it all by saying, 'I am the Lord your God who brought you out of bondage.' Sure, I can understand a redeeming, delivering, liberating God. But a jealous God? Isn't this a bit off base? A God who will not tolerate any rivals? What are we to make of this commandment?"

Certainly, we can understand the prohibition of idols, those fanciful images of things, powers and animals that man makes with his own hands and then worships. We know that to substitute things and idols for the true God is wrong, but those days are largely gone, at least for us. We don't carve graven images any more.

But have we also outgrown this concept of a jealous God?

Could this be one of those ancient ideas of God which is overruled by Jesus' teaching: "You have heard it said by them of old, but I say unto you. . . ."

The New Testament And Jealousy

The answer is "no." The New Testament does not agree with our modern tendency to water down the character of God because we are repelled by the idea of a jealous God. Instead the New Testament has much to say about the judgment of God and the jealousy of God.

Paul writes in Romans 11:22, "Consider therefore the kindness and sternness of God. . . ." We often overlook this because in the New Testament God is like a great heavenly Father, even to the wayward prodigal son. But he is by no means an indulgent, easygoing 20th-century parent who doesn't know what it means to discipline his children. The New Testament also pictures a jealous God who tolerates no rival for the throne of our hearts. God has enemies, yes, but no rivals.

Did you ever realize that there is a striking similarity between what are perhaps the Lord's first commandments in Exodus and the prohibition in perhaps the last commandment in inspired Scripture? As we've seen, the first two commandments prohibit idolatry. Then in the last verse of the last chapter of 1 John, which we know is one of the last and maybe THE last of all of the New Testament writings, we read: "Dear children, keep yourselves from idols." It is amazing that this commandment, seemingly unnecessary for us, is stated in one form or another by the biblical writers more than any other single commandment. Why? Because God knows the human heart. He recognizes the strange and terrible fascination we have for idolatry, our temptation to worship something of our own creation.

An idol is anything or anyone that usurps the place of God in our hearts. The first commandment condemns the worship of all false gods. The second commandment condemns making an image or worshiping an image of any kind, even one of the true God. The first commandment has to do with the unity of God; it tells us *whom* to worship. The second commandment has to do with the spirituality of God; it tells us *how* to worship him in spirit and in truth. This is what God is jealous for; this is what he wants more than anything else.

The word "jealous" in the Old Testament has its roots in the same word as "zealous." We don't need to be afraid of that word. Rather, we should rejoice in it. It shows God's great concern for his children, his white-hot passion, the heart of his nature. He is jealous of his good name, jealous to maintain his covenant, jealous for us to properly understand who he really is.

Why is God's jealousy emphasized in the Old Testament? Because God knew the time was coming when he would fully reveal himself. No longer would people have a partial revelation, a vision here, a word there. No longer would he speak to us as he did in times past through prophets. God knew that soon he would fully reveal himself to us on his timetable, his schedule. That's why he is so jealous in the Old Testament that people do not take some half-hearted, half-way, partial image of what he is really like and conjure up a distorted idea of God. He knew that in the fullness of time he would no longer speak to us through someone but as someone—his Son.

Full Worship Of Christ

Paul writes in Colossians 1:15, "He [Jesus] is the image of the invisible God. . . ." And in verse 19, "For God was pleased to have all his fullness dwell in him [Jesus]. . . ." Are you beginning to understand why only this one commandment in the Ten Commandments has such a serious punishment connnected with its violation? No great punishment is foretold for adultery, murder, lying and other crimes. But the jealous God says that worshiping an image will be punished until the third and fourth generation and the person who does it hates him. Why? Because of God's inexorable love for us, he doesn't want us to settle for anything less than the full worship of Jesus Christ.

Christ alone is the true image, the true person of God. He alone can be worshiped. He alone is worthy of our total commitment. Everything else, anything else, however religious, however fine, we are forbidden to worship. Why? Because not until we see Jesus do we see the Father. Things that the prophets didn't see, Jesus said. Things they wanted to know have been revealed to us. God had to be jealous. He had to be strict to ensure that we would not settle for even the loftiest concepts of him until he'd given us the last word on himself. His word become flesh in Jesus Christ.

Inner Image

The tragedy of the Jewish people living in New Testament times was that they worshiped an inner image of God. It was not an outer graven image, not an idol, for they were long past the days when Aaron made the golden calf and when the ancient kings returned to idolatry again and again. The prophets had come, the exile was over, and they were purified from all of that. They had fought and died to keep that kind of idolatry out of Israel. But they did worship an inner image, a man-made idea of what God was supposed to be like. When God came in the person of his Son, instead of smashing their false man-made image they kept it. Instead they smashed Jesus and crucified him.

But what does the second commandment's stern

warning mean to us? Is it relevant to us who worship
the true and living God, who say we have no other gods
before us? After all, we believe with all of our hearts
that Jesus Christ alone is the true image in the right
biblical sense of the word, the image of the living God.
How could we possibly violate the second commandment?

Using What Should Be Worshiped
I think it is helpful to look at a famous ancient definition of idolatry. Augustine said, "Idolatry is worshiping anything that ought to be used or using anything
that ought to be worshiped." This profound insight
helps us see that the first two commandments are really telling us: "Don't worship anything that is meant
to be used. Don't turn anything, however noble or good
or lovely or wonderful, that God has given to you as a
means to an end, into an end in itself." But how easily
we do this.

Some idols are obvious, such as the material means
of our lives, our possessions. Our clothes, homes, money
and cars are meant to be used as servants, as means to
an end. And yet we often put them first in our lives and
give them top priority, our ultimate devotion and allegiance.

But other things in life become idols too. Knowledge
and wisdom can be worshiped. Sex is another of God's
great gifts, bringing love, children, pleasure and joy.
But how easily we turn this gift, which is meant to be
used, into an all-consuming passion of life. Or we may
worship society, government, a political party, science;
the list is endless. All means can so easily become our
ends. These things are meant to be our servants, but
when they become deified—become ends in themselves—we become their servants and slaves.

Christians are not immune from temptation. Even

the elements of our Christian faith can become idolatrous. These can become the graven images of the Christian life. The greatest illustration of this is the brazen serpent in the Old Testament. When the children of Israel were wandering in the desert, God commanded them to fashion a bronze serpent so they could look at it and be saved. That serpent was the symbol of the saving life and the cross of Jesus Christ. It was an instrument of salvation, something to help deliver the people (see Numbers 21:4-9 and John 3:14-15). But the Israelites began to worship it. It assumed greater and greater significance. This went on until 700 years later when good King Hezekiah came to the throne and began to battle his subjects' paganism and idolatry. As 2 Kings 18:4 tells us, one of the first things Hezekiah did in his great reformation was to break into pieces the bronze serpent that Moses had made, "for up to that time the Israelites had been burning incense to it." A good thing, a God-given thing, a God-ordained means of salvation, had become an idol which was worshiped!

"Christian Idols"
How easy it is to do this with various things in the Christian life, whether the sacrament of baptism, holy communion, church membership, a particular form of worship, lack of a form of worship, precious words, ideas or even doctrines. I know people to whom the doctrine of eternal security or the doctrine of holiness have become idols. The gift of tongues or an experience of some kind can also become idolatrous, assuming a disproportionate role in our lives. When we worship what is meant to be a means of grace we turn it into a graven image. When this happens, we are not only worshiping what ought to be used, but we are also using God. We think we've got God on a leash, where we can manipulate and use him for our own purposes. We must be care-

ful every day, hour and moment not to fall into the temptation of idolatry even at the heart of our Christian life.

Some people even make idols out of their churches. Certain great preachers, whom I believe the Spirit of God has been upon in the past, have brought dishonor upon the name of the living God. I don't doubt that God can still use them, because he uses what he can get, even you and me. But the actions of these renowned television evangelists have made a great travesty of the Christian faith recently—you've read the sordid headlines. However, the poor judgment, sexual misconduct and financial mismanagement of these fallen preachers are not new but common to every generation.

You and I must be careful in our daily Christian lives to avoid worshiping that which is meant to be merely an instrument, a means of grace. If we are not careful we may begin to use the almighty God—who will not allow us to use him—to manipulate him for our own ends, our own honor and glory.

Have you allowed something good in your life, something God-given, intended for use according to his laws and subservient to his love, to become your first priority? If so, it is now an idol in your life. This something could be your possessions, a friend, sweetheart, husband, wife or child. It could be a habit, a talent, a position or a very part of your faith itself.

"Have You Given Your All?"

Perhaps you have heard how F. B. Meyer was led into his deeper experience of the Holy Spirit. The great C. T. Studd said to Meyer one day, "Meyer, have you been filled with the Spirit? Have you given your all to Christ?"

And quickly, too quickly, Meyer said, "Oh, yes, of course."

Studd replied, "Have you turned over every key of

your life to the lordship of Jesus Christ?"

"Oh, yes," Meyer said, "Every key."

But Meyer couldn't sleep that night. He tossed and turned. Two words ran through his mind. Each tick of the clock seemed to say, "Every key, every key, every key." *What is it, Lord? Don't you have the key to every door of every closet of every room of my life?*

Toward dawn of that sleepless night the Holy Spirit laid his hand on one key: F. B. Meyer's power to preach the gospel. Meyer realized he had never really surrendered that to Jesus Christ. *But Lord, You want me to use this.* "Give me the key," said the Spirit. "Every key. Even your power to preach." That was the crisis in F.B. Meyer's life.

No Competition

God will tolerate no rivals, not even our service, not even our concern, not even our white-hot passion, not even our ability, though we live or die for the cause of Jesus Christ. God wants every key. God is zealous that there be no competition. He will not share the throne of our hearts. It is a solitary throne. He wants to look at us and say, "There go my children. They are all mine. They belong to me totally—every part of their personalities, every relationship, every ambition, every desire of life."

When the British divided the great sub-continent of India between India and Pakistan in 1946, they thought they had solved a problem. Instead, they created a thousand more. Overnight India was plunged into a great bloodbath as Hindus and Muslims began to fight and kill one another. All the Hindus living in the North in Pakistan suddenly wanted to get back to India, and all the Muslims in the South wanted to return to their homeland in Pakistan. When they met on the border literally hundreds of thousands, perhaps a million people, died in the carnage.

My good friend Cliff Robinson, a Quaker missionary, was serving in Calcutta at that time, and he told me a tragic story. One day law and order broke down completely on the streets of Calcutta. In the section where Cliff was living, a vast group of young Muslims formed a kind of radical revolutionary army and seized control of that area, which was predominately a Hindu part of town. Cliff and his wife Betty watched from the third floor of their apartment as the mob came down the street. The angry Muslims went from house to house, pulling out the people and beating them, often killing them in cold blood.

A Red Cross
Suddenly they came to a street where a group of Christians were living. They were personal friends of Cliff, four Christian families living side by side in four little apartments. In those days we Christians painted a huge red cross on our house or car or door to tell everybody, "Leave us out of this, we are not Hindu, we are not Muslim." (Because of this, the Christians were able to do a great deal of social service, becoming the medical and relief teams all over India.) And so these four Christian families had huge red crosses painted on their front doors.

As the young Mohammedans came down the street they stopped in front of the first door with a red cross. Cliff couldn't hear them, the noise being too great, but he could see that they were talking with one another. They reached the second apartment, and eventually passed by that door with the red cross on it, as they also did at the fourth door. But at the third door the young men in the army began quite an argument. Suddenly one of the leaders bashed that door open and rushed into that home despite the red cross. They pulled out the screaming occupants, men, women and children, and slaughtered them right there on the streets with their swords. Cliff couldn't figure it out. The first door with the cross was all right, the second door was all right, the fourth door was all right. What was so different about that third door? It had the same cross, but those people were killed.

After law and order was restored, Cliff began to investigate. He learned that the people who lived in that third home were carpenters by trade. Although they were Christians, they had been carving Hindu idols on the side and selling them in the bazaar to make a little extra money. When those fierce monotheistic Muslims, who spit at the very sight of an idol, heard that those so-called Christians had carved Hindu idols, they said, "They're not Christians. We don't care what they profess. They have idols in their homes, and they deserve to die." So they wiped out the household.

Your Heart's Priority

It's a sad story but one that is enacted in many of our lives. We have a cross on the door and claim that the true and living God rules our lives, but we have allowed an idol to become our priority. As the second commandment says, we must not make an idol of anything, even something good. Idolatry is worshiping that which should be used or using that which should be worshiped.

Is there an idol in your heart? Can Christ look down into your heart and say, "There is a rival for my claim over your total personality. You're not all mine"?

"Little children, beware of idols." The Lord your God is a jealous God who will tolerate no rival.

5

What's In A Name?

You shall not misuse the name of the Lord your God, for the Lord will not hold anyone guiltless who misuses his name (Exodus 20:7).

This is how you should pray: "Our Father in heaven, hallowed be your name" (Matthew 6:9).

In the last chapter we saw that the wording of the first and second commandments is perfect, demonstrating the truly divine origin of the commands. The same is true about the order in which we find the Ten Commandments.

Many moderns think the commandments' sequence is all wrong because the ethical or horizontal commandments, the last six, are really the most important. The first four commandments, the vertical ones, are often considered not as vital. They're just relics of ancient myths and superstition, the argument goes, and unnecessary to good relations in daily life.

Dr. Elton Trueblood tells about a survey conducted by several university professors. They asked their students to reorganize the Ten Commandments in what they perceived as the correct order of importance. Some 90 percent of the students opted to reverse the biblical order. But Jesus, who reiterated the greatest and most important commandments, confirms the rightness of

the original order. That's why the third commandment
is in the right place. It belongs near the top because
when Jesus restates it positively, as he did with all the
commandments except the fourth one, he puts it right
at the top. We find it as the very first petition in the
Lord's prayer: "Our Father, hallowed be your name."

At one time this third commandment was merely
emphasized in its negative form as a prohibition
against using God's name as a curse word. There is a
lot more to this commandment, but that's a good
starting place. On its simplest level of meaning it is certainly a command against misusing and profaning the
name of God. The Hebrews themselves took this as one
interpretation of the commandment. Leviticus 19:12
says, "Do not swear falsely by my name and so profane
the name of your God. I am the Lord." The two crimes
which violate this command are perjury and
blasphemy; both were punishable by death under the
Mosaic law.

"Damn Is Not God's Last Name"
In an airport restroom, amid the crude graffiti that
one finds on the walls in such places, one scrawl caught
my attention. It said: "Damn is not God's last name."

Some people today seem to think their vocabulary is
not quite complete unless it is enriched by swear words.
They think the only way to liven up their conversation
is to punctuate it with vigorous oaths. Many of our modern novels, movies and plays spread this dirty virus. I
feel sorry for youngsters, who are perhaps the most sus-
ceptible to this. They want to appear older and more
sophisticated, and they begin using these words. But
plenty of educated and seemingly intelligent people also
talk as if they had been to hell for a post-graduate
course with the devil as their speech instructor.

I remember that I absorbed some strong language

when I was a youngster. I filed it in the back of my mind for future use and thought I was very smart. However, one day it came out when I was very angry. I made the sad mistake of using it on, of all people, my mother. But that wasn't my worst mistake. My worst mistake was that my dad was standing nearby.

Dad, who seemed very calm and quiet, reacted with amazing rapidity. I can still hear his sharp words today: "David, march up those stairs." The history books say Chuck Yeager first exceeded the speed of sound in 1947, but don't you believe it. That night I reached the speed of sound flying up those stairs with my dad right behind me. I could see out of the corner of my eye that he was taking off his belt as he walked. I got one of the worst lickings of my life that night. Dad didn't punish me very often, but when he did it was quite memorable. That night left a lasting impression on my foundation, both physical and moral. And it cured me of an interest in profanity at an early age.

Profaning God's Name

The word "profane" comes from the Latin *pro*, in front of, and *fane*, the temple. Those who use profanity have taken the holy and the sacred out of the temple and allowed their hearts, their minds and their mouths to become a common marketplace.

Why do people use God's name as a common oath? Is it because they are so familiar with God? Or could they just want to use his name all the time? No, exactly the opposite is true. Those who use God's name as a swear word are not really on speaking terms with him. Do you know anyone who communes deeply with God, who is close to God and who has the habit of misusing his name? Of course not. The person who learns true reverence knows God's name is the doorway to the audience chamber of the Lord.

Our daughter once told me about watching Merv Griffin interview Charlton Heston. He's the famous actor who played the part of Moses in "The Ten Commandments" and also starred in "Ben Hur." Merv Griffin asked Charlton Heston if any of the characters he had portrayed in his religious movies had changed his spiritual outlook. Heston didn't answer the question directly. He thought a moment and then simply said, "Well, Merv, you can't walk barefoot down Mount Sinai and be the same person you were when you went up." You can't, can you? You can't get close to God, know him intimately and then toss his name around lightly. Carelessly and thoughtlessly using his name will prevent you from that reverence that brings about intimacy and communion with God.

Awe Of Yahweh

The Jews wouldn't even pronounce God's name— they held it in such awe. Even when writing it, a copyist was fearfully cautious. First he'd bathe and don full Jewish dress. He'd never dip his pen in the ink in the middle of writing the name of God. Indeed if a king addressed him while he was writing the name of Yahweh, the copyist would ignore him completely.

While I lived in India some older missionaries told me a story about the great missionary named Praying Hyde. Praying Hyde was on very intimate terms with God. Once when he was at a missionary meeting with a circle of friends, someone called on him to pray. Everybody bowed their heads, including Hyde. There was a long pause that seemed to last for a minute or more. The man who had asked him to pray began to wonder whether Hyde had heard the request, so he opened his eyes and looked over at him. But he decided not to say anything because Hyde had his head bowed. Finally this great man said just two words: "O, God." And there was another long pause. The missionaries who were there say that the way he expressed those two words brought a holy hush upon the prayer meeting. Everyone there felt as if they had been taken by the hand and ushered into the very presence of the living God.

God will not hold us guiltless when we toss about his name carelessly and profanely.

Insincerity

On another level, this third commandment is a prohibition against insincerity of speech, perjury, false promises and the breaking of our word. Early in human history people came to lie so frequently that no one could trust a person's ordinary word. In order to be believed one had to call upon God to witness to the truth. We think the coverups and evasions going on today in the political arena and elsewhere are modern phenomena, but the problem is really as old as humanity. The idea also emerged that if you did not swear by God, then you didn't have to tell the truth. But gradually people became such liars that even that didn't help. People felt that unless they took a certain complex oath they were not obligated to tell the truth.

By the time Jesus came along the situation was terrible. People used all kinds of oaths and still lied. It was impossible to tell whether they told the truth, even though they took the name of God. That's why Jesus said, "Do not swear at all. . . . Simply let your 'Yes' be 'Yes' and your 'No,' 'No'. . . ." (Matthew 5:34, 37). Jesus is saying that we shouldn't have to be put under oath to tell the truth because, if that's the case, we would probably still lie even though we had taken the oath.

I remember a fellow who came by my office early in my pastorate in Wilmore, Kentucky. He told me a story about a relative who had died, leaving no money for the funeral. It was quite a sob story, and I really didn't believe it. But he nagged me so much that I did something I didn't often do. I gave him some money. He was very grateful and promised me that it was just a loan and that after the funeral he'd come back and work for me. He looked out the window at my car and said, "I'll wash your car to repay you for this kindness."

Somehow, I didn't care for his story, I wasn't in a very good mood and I said a rather unkind thing: "Now, you be sure to do that because if you do you'll be the first person in all my years to keep your word this way. No one has ever come back to repay me, and I would like to see you break my record."

He was deeply pained by my words. I had wounded him. Tears came to his eyes, and he raised his right hand. He said, "I will come back and wash your car, and if I don't I pray that God will strike me dead." That must be exactly what happened because I never laid eyes on him again!

When we use God's name in oaths we give the impression that we are binding ourselves by our words. But one doesn't need to utter an oath to break it. As Christians, we bear the name of Christ in our name, meaning that we belong to him. We've accepted his name as our name, but some of us take that name in vain. We profane it by breaking our word.

Carelessness, Unfaithfulness And Perjury

Some of us profane the name of our Lord by our carelessness in borrowing money and failing to repay it, in running up bills with no intention of ever paying them back. Some of us profane God's name by being unfaithful to our marriage vows, the sacred oaths made as husbands and wives that are often broken by lustful, unfaithful living. Some of us profane his name because we stood at the altar of a church and said we would be faithful to the church, support it and be loyal to it. Yet we break that vow. Some parents profane the name of God by breaking vows they took at the baptism of their children, when they promised God they would nurture and discipline those children in private and public worship. And some of us come to church for years, listen to sermons, sing songs and drink the cup of communion, but our lips speak his name in vain because we lie to ourselves about our lives. We perjure ourselves with the oaths we take.

The third commandment is vital because perfect truthfulness is Christ's standard. Let us say "yes" and mean "yes" and "no" and mean "no." That is why one of the deeper meanings of the third commandment is that Christians who take the name of Christ should not profane it by failing to live up to our word and our obligations.

But this commandment has an even more profound meaning. The third commandment also warns against the misuse of God's power. In this sense it is a practical extension of the first and second commandments.

God's Name, God's Character

Remember that in the Old and New Testaments a name was believed to be a mysterious part of one's personality, an extension of one's character. Similarly, throughout the Scriptures God's name represents the nature and character of God himself. So to speak for God is to speak in his name (Deuteronomy 18:19, 20). To praise God is to praise his name (Psalms 96:2; Psalms 100:4). To worship God is to call upon the name of God (Genesis 4:26; Isaiah 64:7). To serve God is to love his name (Psalm 5:11). The temple for God's worship is the "place the Lord your God will choose. . .to put his Name" (Deuteronomy 12:5). "Those who know your name will trust in You. . ." (Psalms 9:10). To know the name of God is in some way to know the power of God.

Acts 4:7 tells how the religious leaders questioned Peter and John about their healing of the lame man, asking, "By what power or what name did you do this?" And Peter answered, "It is by the name of Jesus Christ of Nazareth. . ." (Acts 4:10). Eventually the high court angrily let them go, warning the apostles "not to speak or teach at all in the name of Jesus" (Acts 4:18).

You see, God's name includes his character, his will, his power. That's why we are to pray in the name of Christ and why God's name has special power and meaning for us. The third commandment is saying, "Be very careful. Don't use the name of God for your own selfish ends. Don't attempt to use God's power for your own will and your own ways. Don't try to sign God's name to a lot of things in your life that are utterly unworthy of his name."

The Stamp Of Approval

But how easy it is to do precisely that. In our prayers, for example, we often present our life plans and then piously ask God to bless them. Or we may choose our life's mate knowing down deep that our choice is not acceptable to God. Often the person is not even a Christian, and Scripture very plainly says that choice is against God's will. Nevertheless we take our choice to God like a bill of sale and say, "Please, Lord, put your rubber stamp on this; put your name and your approval on my choice."

Simon, the magician in Acts 8, watched the apostles lay their hands upon new converts and the Holy Spirit enter those people. Jesus had said, "You will receive power when the Holy Spirit comes on you. . ." (Acts 1:8). But when Simon saw this happen he did not say, "Give me the Holy Spirit." He said, "Give me this power." He wanted to reverse Christ's divine order (the Holy Spirit comes first, then the power). Peter rebuked Simon

severely, saying, "You have no part or share in this ministry, because your heart is not right before God. Repent
of this wickedness and pray to the Lord" (Acts 8:21-22).

How many of our prayers for sanctification and the
power of the Holy Spirit are really motivated by our
desire to do great things for God to impress other
people? How often do we pray for some special gift so
that we can join a spiritually elite corps and say, "See
what God has done for me"? Simon the magician wanted
power for magic not miracle. God does not lease his
power out to people apart from his moral person and
characteristics. When we pray, "Oh, Lord, fill me with
your Holy Spirit" we are praying for the miracle of fullness which brings the power of God.

Can God trust us with his name and his power?
What would we do with power if God gave it to us today?
Would we take his name in vain, profane it and use it
for our own ends, our own glory? Before we can be
trusted with his name and his power we must first fully
surrender *our* names and spiritual reputations into his
hands.

Honoring His Name
That leads us to our final thought. This commandment, this ancient God-given prohibition, "You shall not
misuse the name of the Lord your God" is only really
fulfilled in a positive way, as in the Lord's prayer: "Hallowed be your name." The Old Testament states the
commandment negatively: "Don't unhallow the name of
God, don't besmirch it, don't misuse it, don't drag it
down." Jesus was saying, "Hallowed be the name of
God." The Phillips translation of that verse is, "Let your
name be honored."

What's in a name? Plenty. When an explorer enters
a new territory the first thing he or she does is to hoist
a flag in the name of the king, queen or country, claim-

ing the discovery in that name and in that authority.

What's in a name? A lot. A well-known company that wants to sell you its business for $5 million might say, "If you want to continue using our company's name, the price is $10 million." Why? Because on the sales market that company's good name is worth another $5 million.

What's in a name? Everything. Does your life profane his name? Or does it hallow his name and honor his name? Can a servant who works for a family bring honor or dishonor to that family's name? Of course not. Only a member of the family can honor or dishonor a family name. Beloved, we are called by his name. We are his children, "co-heirs with Christ" (Romans 8:17).

In the Bible God's name is a key to his essential nature and his true character. To pray "Hallowed be your name" is to be committed to the character of Jesus Christ, to his nature, to his will for us and for the world.

In your mind's eye, examine your life for a moment. With risking and ruthless honesty, search your innermost heart, your deepest motives, your attitudes toward other people. Then ask yourself, can God sign his holy name to them? Now look at your daily schedule, your routine, your list of priorities. Can God sign his holy name under that list? Now look at your body, the temple of the Holy Spirit, the instrument of your personality for sin or for righteousness. Scrutinize your recreation, sex life, service, work, diet, even the way you drive your car. Review the way you live and use your body, your hands, your feet, your mind. Can God sign his name to every activity of your physical temple? The list is endless isn't it? How about your money? Does God co-sign his holy name on your checkbook? What about your home, your habits, your mood, your manners, your deeds, your disposition? Can God sign his name to our lives? Do our lives honor his holy name? If so, we are keeping the third commandment.

6

The Sabbath: Holy Day Or Holiday?

Remember that you were slaves in Egypt and that the Lord your God brought you out of there with a mighty hand and an outstretched arm. Therefore the Lord your God has commanded you to observe the Sabbath day (Deuteronomy 5:15).

Thus far we've been trying to discover what value the Ten Commandments have for us in our modern age. To do this we've examined not only the original Old Testament commandment, but also how it is reinterpreted and restated in the New Testament in the light of the gospel of Jesus Christ. Of all the commandments, we especially need to do this with the fourth one. If we don't, we might become very confused.

Let me illustrate this with a story from California. A young lady who lived there had never learned to drive a car. However when she got a job she knew she had to learn to drive. As anyone who has been in California knows, finding a highway where an inexperienced driver can safely practice is no easy task. Finally a friend suggested, "Why don't you get up early on Sunday morning, say between six and seven o'clock, and go out on the freeway. At that hour it will be relatively empty. The Protestants will be in bed sleeping, the

Catholics will be at Mass and the rest will be on the golf course, so you'll have nothing to worry about." Well, she took his suggestion and got along fine until she had an accident one Sunday morning a few weeks later. What happened? She was hit by a Seventh Day Adventist in a hurry to get to work.

Sabbath Misunderstandings

A lot of confusion, misunderstanding, dogmatism and hard feelings are generated by this commandment. Almost everybody uses it to prove some point of view. So let's move very carefully as we explore what it means to observe the Sabbath today.

Let's begin with the ancient commandment itself. As it stands literally, it was a commandment given to the Hebrew people to set apart the seventh day of the week, the Sabbath, as a day of total rest. In its original form in Exodus, it merely forbade the performance of work on the seventh day, which would be Saturday. In this sense it was a specific Jewish commandment and part of the ancient covenant. Taken in the very literal sense the commandment does not have a great deal of meaning for Christians in a day of grace.

Let's say it plainly and in complete honesty. Our Sunday, the first day of the week, is not the same day as Saturday, the seventh day. Sabbath means the seventh, and the Sabbath day was Saturday, the seventh day. But we are Christians, not Jews; most of us are not even Christian Jews. In our Christian vocabulary of hymns and poems we certainly can use the word "Sabbath" as a valid figure of speech when referring to Sunday. But we should understand that the two are not the same.

This fourth commandment is the only Old Testament commandment that is not repeated anywhere in the New Testament. All the other Old Testament commandments are reiterated and often made more stringent in the New Testament. But not this one. There is no record of Jesus teaching anyone to keep the Sabbath. As far as we know, no apostle ever told anyone to keep it. In John 5:18 we're told in plain words that Jesus broke the Sabbath, and in this and other stories we almost get the impression that he did so deliberately.

Acts 15:19-31 describes the first great church conference, the Jerusalem council, when the apostles and elders sent instructions to the new Gentile Christians. Significantly, although they gave several rules, they did not mention the need to keep the Sabbath. Also, the two most Jewish books in the New Testament, Hebrews and James, do not restate the Sabbath law in any form.

In all of the New Testament's lists of sins, Sabbath-breaking is never mentioned. In fact the reverse is true. In Galatians 4:10-11 Paul condemns making the Sabbath a law. Paul also writes in Colossians 2:16-17, "Therefore do not let anyone judge you by what you eat or drink, or with regard to a religious festival, a New Moon celebration or a Sabbath day. These are a shadow of the things that were to come; the reality, however, is found in Christ."

Jesus' Sabbath Teaching

The writers of the New Testament were certainly consistent with Jesus' teaching in Matthew 12:1-14.

At that time Jesus went through the grainfields on the Sabbath. His disciples were hungry and began to pick some heads of grain and eat them. When the Pharisees saw this, they said to him, "Look! Your disciples are doing what is unlawful on the Sabbath."

He answered, "Haven't you read what David did when he and his companions were hungry? He entered the house of God, and he and his companions ate the consecrated bread—which was not lawful for them to do, but only for the priests. Or haven't you read in the Law that on the Sabbath the priests in the temple desecrate the day and yet are innocent? I tell you that one greater than the temple is here. If you had known what these words mean, 'I desire mercy, not sacrifice,' you would not have condemned the innocent. For the Son of Man is Lord of the Sabbath."

Going on from that place, he went into their synagogue, and a man with a shriveled hand was there. Looking for a reason to accuse Jesus, they asked him, "Is it lawful to heal on the Sabbath?"

He said to them, "If any of you has a sheep and it falls into a pit on the Sabbath, will you not take hold of it and lift it out? How much more valuable is a man than a sheep! Therefore it is lawful to do good on the Sabbath."

Then he said to the man, "Stretch out your hand." So he stretched it out and it was completely restored, just as sound as the other. But the Pharisees went out and plotted how they might kill Jesus.

Jesus placed the literal seventh day (Saturday) Sabbath observance with the rest of the Jewish ceremonial law. Like the whole sacrificial system, he did not make it binding upon us. But if the *letter* of the law, the seventh day Sabbath, is not applicable to us today, certainly the *principle* of the Sabbath still is. For it is grounded in the nature of God, in the nature of man and in the nature of the universe itself.

It's the Principle That Counts

Although the New Testament nowhere echoes the exact literal Saturday Sabbath command, it certainly does reinforce the divine principle behind that command. This principle of the Sabbath is that a specific and proportionate amount of time is to be hallowed, to be set apart for rest and for worship.

This idea existed long before the fourth commandment was etched on the stone tablets of Moses. This divine principle does not appear first in Exodus but in the first chapter of Genesis, which tells how God himself rested after six days of creative labor. Also, while the Hebrew people wandered in the wilderness before Moses received the tablets on Mt. Sinai, the principle of the Sabbath was reflected in the way God sent his people the life-sustaining manna. On the sixth day the people were to gather a double portion of manna because none was sent on the seventh, the Sabbath day.

The Sabbath principle is that we need one day of rest and worship after six days of labor. We must observe a seventh day, not necessarily *the* seventh day, which is Saturday. Remember that the day of atonement in the Old Testament was called a Sabbath. Yet the day of atonement was on the tenth day of the seventh month, not the seventh day. So the word "Sabbath" was not restricted to just the seventh day.

Dropping Saturday

The Christians of the New Testament soon discarded the literal seventh day, or Saturday, Sabbath but kept the Sabbath-day principle. They stopped celebrating a Saturday Sabbath and instead began keeping the first day of the week, which is our Sunday, as a day of rest and worship. This was done under the authority of the apostles, Christ's appointed teachers.

The early Christians celebrated on Sunday, the first day of the week, because it is the day Christ arose from the dead. Paul follows his great resurrection chapter, 1 Corinthians 15, with the 16th chapter which says in verse 2, "On the first day of every week, each one of you should set aside a sum of money in keeping with his income..." to be used for God's work. So Paul establishes a principle of giving a time and proportionate gift or tithe to God.

In Revelation 1:10, John writes, "On the Lord's day I was in the Spirit. . . ." Perhaps that's a more fitting name for a day of rest and worship than Sunday or Sabbath. I wish all Christians would get in the habit of calling it the Lord's day, which celebrates his resurrection.

But it's not enough to simply know how we got our Sunday or our Lord's day. We need to understand why this command is still binding upon us. We find the key in three places in Scripture.

❖ First, in Exodus 20:8-11 the command to keep the Sabbath day holy is based on the fact that God rested on the seventh day after working six days tocreate everything. He has built this pattern into all of us.

❖ Second, in Deuteronomy 5:15 the command is restated and an entirely new reason is given for remembering the Sabbath day: "Remember that you were slaves in Egypt and that the Lord your God brought you out of there with a mighty hand. . . . Therefore the Lord your God has commanded you to observe the Sabbath day."

❖ Third, in Mark 2:27-28 Jesus says, "The Sabbath was made for man, not man for the Sabbath. So the Son of man is Lord even of the Sabbath."

Now let's examine these three biblical references, beginning with the last, "The Sabbath was made for man." In other words, the divine principle of a fixed proportionate time for rest and worship is one of God's greatest gifts to us. It was not created for God's benefit but for ours.

Need Of Man, Character Of God

Let's think about this in conjunction with the verses in Exodus that say that the Sabbath is rooted in the nature of God himself; God worked six days, then rested one. Jesus says the Sabbath is rooted in the nature and needs of man. Are these assertions contradictory? No. As we've seen in previous chapters, the commandments emerge from the character of God. Man is made in the image of God. Therefore both propositions are true. The

Sabbath principle comes from the nature of God, and since we are made in his pattern and image the Sabbath is naturally appropriate and fitting to our needs too.

One of the basic principles of personality, whether the divine or the human, is the need for rhythmic alteration between work and rest. God worked creatively for six days, then He rested for the seventh. This fourth commandment is not only written on tablets of stone but also on the tablets of our hearts, our bodies, our emotions and our minds. This law is written into every cell of the human body.

If we are to thrive, we must learn that the Sabbath principle is one of the moral laws of the universe. This is the way God is and this is the way the universe is. The rhythm of life comes from the rhythmic throbbing of the heart of God himself. The tides rise and fall. Day alternates with night. The seasons change—the dry, the wet, the hot, the cold. Nature has its rhythm: a time for fruit and a time for rest. All of this is regulated by divine law and principle.

A Merciful Gift
A tree can't decide to produce leaves and fruit during the cold, hard months of winter when it must rest. It doesn't have that freedom of choice and action. But you and I do have that freedom, and that's our problem. We can drive our bodies, minds and emotions long past the point of needed rest and recreation. That's because as humans we have the power of choice. We're always in danger of destroying ourselves for some false set of values. Because of this hazard, God in his mercy gave us a great gift—a Sabbath day, a day set apart, the Lord's day, a day of rest and worship, relaxation, recuperation and joy.

It's astounding how this divine principle has been

proven over and over to be medically and psychologically sound. For example, a Dr. Hagler of Switzerland once conducted a series of experiments about oxygen and the human body. He discovered that our bodies expend more oxygen in a day of toil than they recover in a night of rest. A weekly day of rest is necessary to restore the cumulative loss of oxygen from our six days of labor. Sir James C. Brown, a famous British doctor, once said, "We doctors in the treatment of nervous diseases are now constantly compelled to prescribe periods of rest. Some periods are, I think, only Sundays in arrears."

After the French revolution, the French people were trying to sever all their past ties with religion and the church. An anti-God and anti-church spirit of rebellion captured the land. They decided to abolish the weekly Sunday and decreed that one out of every 10 days should be a day of rest. The experiment was so disastrous that despite the strong anti-religious feelings, government officials had to reinstate Sunday, one day out of seven, as a day of rest.

Salute To The Sabbath

If you ever visit beautiful Hennepin Avenue United Methodist Church in Minneapolis, you'll notice the church's exquisite ascension window in the sanctuary. It was given in memory of one of the leading families of several generations ago in that church, the family of Hugh Galbraith Harrison. A brochure kept in a special place in front of the church tells the story of that family, and one of its stories is very interesting.

In 1850 Mr. Harrison's family, lured by the great gold rush, decided to move to California by wagon train. Being deeply religious Methodists they decided not to travel on Sundays, which were to be strictly days of rest, Bible reading and worship. Of course, while they were

parked on Sunday, scores of wagon trains would pass
them. Other travelers made comments like, "Pious
fools, you may have all the gold on the streets of heaven,
but you won't get any of the gold in California because
we'll get there first." Nevertheless the Harrison wagon
train not only caught up with the others but eventually
passed them and arrived first. What's more, they and
their animals were in sound, healthy condition.

The Sabbath is a medical law that began in creation.
It is rooted in the heart of God and in the needs of
mankind. So the general principle we should follow is
something like this: We should not do on Sunday what
we are able to finish on any other day.

Two Extremes

Throughout history the observance of the Sabbath
has inspired two extremes. People have found ways to
misuse this gift, just as they misuse God's other gifts.

One group of people has historically made Sunday a
day of gloom and depression instead of a day of joy and
gladness. This is what had happened by Jesus' time.
Those law-happy rabbis had counted 39 letters in
Moses' commandment. They had multiplied 39 by 39
and come up with the number 1,521. Believe it or not,
by the time Jesus came along, they had defined 1,521
possible ways to break the Sabbath. Some of these vi-
olations are downright amusing, but they are all rather
tragic.

Some Christians have gone to similar extremes.
Years ago in New England a Boston sea captain returned home after a two-year voyage. His wife ran out
to the gate and kissed him, welcoming him home. She
was promptly put into prison because she had forgotten
that it was Sunday.

We don't make our witness winsome when we turn
this commandment into something like, "Thou shalt not

enjoy life on Sunday." Many of us mean well, but we cannot make people, especially children, enjoy God by forbidding them to enjoy anything else on Sunday. Such a rigid observance of Sunday can become idolatrous. It had become idolatrous by Jesus' day and that is why he shattered the legalistic Sabbath observance.

Making Sunday A Holiday

But I think our problem today is usually the opposite extreme. We tend to take this holy day and turn it into a holiday, a day of commercialized recreation, entertainment and profit. Some of us have taken that passage where Jesus says that if the ox falls in the ditch on the Sabbath it's all right to pull it out (see Luke 14:5) and turned it into a lot of bull. If we are careful and don't avoid pushing the ox into the pit during the week, we may not have to spend Sunday pulling it out. If your ox has a habit of falling into the same pit every Sunday, it's time you either fill up the pit or get rid of the ox.

Columnist Carl Rowan, in a stinging article in *Eternity* magazine, once wrote:

> Shall we gather at the stadium? Let the Catholics and Protestants fight, let the Republicans and Democrats bicker, maybe they are for real, but the true religion in this country, the only politics that counts in the fall, is professional football. In 26 cities across this land and hundreds of towns nearby the great Sunday loyalty no longer is expressed in fervent singing of "The Old Rugged Cross" but in feverish praise of a rugged front four dealing mayhem to the opposing quarterback. Football worship has not yet taken over Sunday to the extent that we are throwing the Christians to the lions, except perhaps the ones that come from Detroit. Those sensitive millionaires who own pro football even show a certain sense of delicacy by consenting to start their games after what presumably has been Mr. & Mrs. America's attendance at church. But you watch the maddening throng and I suspect that the only prayers

most of those fans utter on Sunday is that Gene Stenarude will miss or make a victory or defeat field goal. You also suspect that, counting the tickets, the booze, the hotdogs, the pennants, and the wagers, a lot more money goes into pro football every Sunday than goes into all those collection plates at the 328,657 churches that dot America. Football is the new religion. The ritual and the pomp are clearly there, the cheerers have their catechism and the superstitions that pervade pro football make a Hottentot witchdoctor look like a super-sophisticate.

I think Carl Rowan is saying something very serious. Sunday has become the day of the athletic contest, the day when the highways are the most crowded, not on the way to church but on the way to the beach, the mountains or the movies. How tragic it is that some of us Christians simply have no convictions about what Sunday ought to be like. Some of us feel this way because we have rebelled against a home that was too strict. But if so we should be prayerful about this rebellion and take a realistic look at the way we keep Sunday or perhaps do not keep it. We may be going to the opposite extreme, which can be just as destructive, and maybe a little more so.

A Day To Remember

Now let's look at the second principle found in Deuteronomy 5:15, "Remember that you were slaves in Egypt and that the Lord your God brought you out of there with a mighty hand. . . . Therefore the Lord your God has commanded you to observe the Sabbath day." The first principle was *rest*. The second principle is *remembrance*. We need Sunday not just because our bodies need resting, but because our spirits need reminding. The command as it appears in Exodus 20:8 begins, "Remember the Sabbath day," and "remember" is the key word. "You were once slaves, but you've been delivered. Therefore, keep this day holy. Remember."

Why? Because it's our sinful nature to forget. You and I need constant reminding. We not only forget the small trivialities of everyday life but also forget the great eternal issues. If we set aside one day in seven as a holy day when we do not do work that we can do on other days, as a day that will refresh our bodies, renew our souls, realign our values and restore our love, then we will remember God. We will make him first in our lives. Let's face it; if we forget and treat that day carelessly, we will surely forget him. If we remember his day we will remember that he delivered us from the slavery of sin. If we forget that we came out of sin we could soon find ourselves back in it.

An Example From History

In 1924 a young Scotsman named Eric Liddel, a great runner, entered the Olympic Games. The race for which he was most famous and was favored to win fell on Sunday. Eric Liddel, a devout Christian, refused to run the race on Sunday. This caused a furor, and he was greatly criticized. Because he lost a point for Britain he practiced for a race that he had never run before, the 200 meters, and won it.

Another young Scotsman followed this story in the newspaper and was deeply influenced by it. In fact, he says it played a major part in his conversion and dedication to the Lord. His name was Peter Marshall. How many people have been won to Christ by his preaching, his books and his wife Catherine's books? Of course, a half-century later millions more were influenced when Liddel's story was made into the movie *Chariots of Fire*. And all because a man remembered to keep the Sabbath holy.

Eric Liddel remembered his Lord. To remember is to witness that Christ is the Lord of time, the Lord of all our lives. God has that reasonable claim on our time.

The Sabbath is also a gracious gift to recreate body and soul. Let us not profane this gift. Let us keep it a holy day, even though others all around us may turn it into a holiday. Let us make it a day of rest and worship and joy. When we do this, the question won't be, "Can I do this on the Lord's day without breaking a law?" The question will be, "If I do this, will I miss a blessing?"

7

God's Family Plan

Honor your father and your mother, so that you may live long in the land the Lord your God is giving you (Exodus 20:12).

Children, obey your parents in the Lord, for this is right. "Honor your father and mother"—which is the first commandment with a promise—"that it may go well with you and that you may enjoy long life on the earth."

Fathers, do not exasperate your children, instead, bring them up in the training and instruction of the Lord (Ephesians 6:1-4).

The fifth commandment in Exodus 20:12 really begins several verses and commandments earlier in Exodus 20:5-6 with some rather startling words: "I, the Lord your God, am a jealous God, punishing the children for the sin of the fathers to the third and fourth generation of those who hate me, but showing love to thousands who love me and keep my commandments." When most of us read those words our minds become filled with false ideas. We conjure up a fearful picture of God sending bolts of lightning, punishment, disease and death. We also feel this is more than a little bit unfair. How can unborn and innocent babies deserve the wrath of an angry God?

But such a picture is totally unnecessary. This com-

mandment deals with the consequences of family behavior. Families are part of God's plan. No one is an is-
land, and "God sets the lonely in families," as Psalms
68:6 tells us. The nature of human life is that each
generation begins where the previous generation places
it. That's not some ancient, pious code. That's an indis-
putable fact of history. This means both the blessings
and the sins of the parents have an impact on succes-
sive generations. This is true genetically, physically,
sociologically, psychologically and spiritually. Each
generation starts where the previous generation leaves
off. And because this is the nature of human society, we
need a commandment to guide us.

Children As Property
To understand God's plan for family life, we'll first
look at the command to "Honor your father and your
mother" in the Old Testament and then explore ways
Jesus and the New Testament writers restated it. The
fifth commandment, as it appears in the Old Testament,
is based on concepts which have changed. In those days
children were viewed as property, more as things than
persons. In the Old Testament children are often listed
as economic assets in an account of a man's property.

Then a father's word was the law. It wasn't under
the law, it *was* the law. When Jephthah made a foolish
vow to sacrifice to the Lord the first thing he saw—and
the first thing happened to be his only child—he stuck
to the vow and sacrificed his daughter (see Judges
11:29-40). The Old Testament never for a moment questioned his right to do it. Parents literally had power of
life and death over their children.

Jesus changed the status of children just as he
changed the status of women. In his eyes they became
persons of value before God. He loved them and blessed
them. But Luke 17:2 contains one of his most severe

warnings to us—that if we do anything to "cause one of these little ones to sin" it would be far better for us to have a millstone put around our necks and to be thrown into the sea.

The old commandment found in Exodus and Deuteronomy is reissued in a beautiful, loving Christian form by the Apostle Paul in Ephesians 6:1-4. Paul broadened the commandment to include both children and parents. We will examine this New Testament form of the commandment to discover what relevance the fifth commandment has for our contemporary society.

The first ingredient of that commandment is discipline, or "training." "Discipline" is not a popular word, but discipline is the very essence of life. Luke 2:41-51 tells us that after the incident when the 12-year-old Jesus left his parents' traveling group to return to the temple in Jerusalem, he became obedient to the authority of his parents. Hebrews 5:7-9 reminds us that Christ himself learned obedience. Some things we cannot choose or obtain; we can only learn them. Discipline and obedience are among those things. This was even true for God himself incarnate in Jesus Christ. We learn discipline by obedience to a higher authority.

Self-Centered Nature

Children by nature are self-centered. They want to be their own gods and run their world the way they would like to. It's up to parents to teach them that the world just doesn't work that way and that if they insist on their own way, they will be hurt very badly. This commandment assumes that parents have learned some things from experience. Young people sometimes don't realize that their parents, who may not have as much formal education as they have, do possess wisdom gained from life experiences. For example, a father said to his early teenage daughter, "Honey, I want you home from your date tonight no later than 11 o'clock."

"But Daddy," she said, "I'm no longer a little child."

"I know," he said, "That's why I want you home by 11 o'clock."

You see, parents learn some things by experience. They learn that this is a moral universe. They learn that the law of gravity always operates and one never breaks it; one only breaks oneself on it. They learn that fire always burns. You can't fool around with some things without getting hurt. Parents learn that certain roads can lead to heaven and other roads are certain to lead to hell.

But many times children refuse to accept these facts. They rebel against their parents' authority. They want to find things out for themselves. Those are the times when discipline is needed.

Ephesians 6:4 says, "Bring them up in the training and instruction of the Lord." The old King James translation "nurture and admonition" is much too weak. The word used in the original Greek is a strong word. The lexicon says that this word "refers to training by act and discipline. It includes not only commands of the mouth but the enforcement of those commands by reproof and punishment if necessary."

"Never Cross A Child"

In recent decades we've experienced a tragic age. We have gone to an idiotic extreme on the whole subject of discipline. "Never cross a child," the modern gurus teach. "Never thwart him. Never punish him. The child must choose for himself." We've forgotten that sometimes a child can only be taught to choose the right option by making the wrong option painful. What happens if a child wants to play with a razor instead of a harmless toy? What happens if a youngster behaves as if the whole world revolves around him? Do we let him grow up thinking he is the center of the universe? The universe takes a dim view of anyone who thinks that he is the center of it.

Let me backtrack a bit at this point. The commandment "Children, obey your parents..." is not isolated in Ephesians 6:1. This passage really begins in Ephesians 5:21, "Submit to one another out of reverence for Christ." God's family plan is a package deal, and it should be understood that way. Who's the boss in the family? Who's in charge of the home? The Bible tells us Jesus Christ is supposed to be. God's family plan begins with a husband and wife mutually submitting to Jesus Christ and to one another because they have made a prior submission to Christ himself (Ephesians 5:22-33). Thus with Paul's model of Christ and his Church as the model for husband-wife relationships, there is self-sacrificing love and a pattern of service as each spouse ministers to the other through the use of his or her particular gifts.

Mutual Submission

It is in this setting of mutual submission and shared responsibility that the children then submit to the authority of their parents. And since husband and wife have both submitted to Christ and to one another the children's submission to the lordship and authority of Christ comes about by submitting to their parents. This is God's pattern of authority, and it is desperately needed in modern families. We have swung from the extremes of two or three generations ago when parents (especially fathers) were unreasonable tyrants to the place where parents (especially fathers) have abdicated their place of authority and responsibility in the home. The pattern of authority is all one piece, and you cannot break it at one place and expect it to work further down the line. "Children, obey your parents in the

Lord," is where we want the chain to work. But it cannot if we have broken the prior links.

Sharing Of Authority

Today, when both parents are often working outside the home, it cannot be overemphasized how important it is for there to be mutual unity and sharing of authority by both parents. Without this the whole family plan is disrupted. We see this in either direction when there is not a united and agreed upon responsibility. One parent may merely become the one who seconds the motion: "You heard what your mother said," or "Wait 'til your dad gets home." Or one becomes the great referrer: "Ask Mom/Dad."

In God's family plan both parents should assume their rightful roles, whatever this may require in time, energy and the redirecting of priorities. If it means cutting back on work or outside interests (including the church activities), then it must be done. In this way parental authority cannot be destroyed by a child's "divide and rule" policy.

But Paul also has a word for parents: "Fathers, do not exasperate your children. . . ." "Don't overcorrect them," says Phillips. Don't goad them into resentment. This shows that love and discipline should exist together, side by side in a beautiful way.

Some young people are not happy with Paul's teaching. A newspaper questionnaire once asked 369 high school boys and 415 high school girls to complete a checklist of the 10 most desirable qualities in a father. Guess what quality received the second highest vote. "Respecting his children's wishes." Following closely on that was "never nagging," "making plenty of money," "being well-dressed" and "owning a good-looking car." This is not quite the biblical ideal.

Many young people come to me with questions on

matters of conviction, and I always tell them that the Scriptures say, "Obey your parents. Respect them." I point out that they will have their own homes some day and will make their own decisions. But at this time the Lord says the way they can best serve God and honor him is by obeying their parents.

Necessity Of Obedience

There's another reason for learning to obey parents: all of our lives we will face the necessity of obedience, subjection and discipline. We may not like our government's laws or the people enforcing those laws, but we're in for a terrible shock if we don't learn obedience and discipline. Anyone can do the things he or she likes to do. The test of character is whether we can do things that we do not like to do.

What happens when we don't learn to obey when we're young? What happens if you haven't learned to discipline yourself, and you get married? What if you've grown up thinking that you can scream or pout or emotionally blackmail the rest of the family to get your own way? What chance does your marriage have? Marriage requires self-control, consideration and discipline. When two people who grew up in undisciplined homes meet in a marriage it's like the proverbial irresistible force meeting the immovable object, usually resulting in catastrophe.

And what about the laws of the land? If you don't learn to obey and respect authority in the home, you won't respect it on the highway or in the community. It will become easy to break state laws because you've never learned submission to higher laws.

Paul adds a qualifying clause to the Old Testament command that's important. "Obey your parents *in the Lord.*" This passage is interpreted two ways. "In the Lord" may mean, "this is the way that you please the

Lord," and some translators render it that way. In other words, a young person obeys the Lord by obeying his or her parents. But I think today there is a broader meaning. Paul has put some limits on the authority of the parents. I know parents who have asked their children to go against their own Christian consciences. Non-Christian parents have tried to coerce children into doing things that are morally wrong. Paul has set limits on authority as a protection. He's made it clear that our highest obedience is to the Lord and that sometimes, though rarely, that could take precedence over obedience to our parents. So the New Testament restatement of the fifth commandment is not just a blank check to parents. It says, "Children, obey your parents *in the Lord.*"

Don't Overdo It

In Ephesians 6:4 Paul also tells parents not to overdo it. Don't provoke your children to anger, don't exasperate them or irritate them. Phillips renders it this way: "Fathers, don't overcorrect your children or make it difficult for them to obey the commandment." I think the New English Bible translation is perhaps best of all: "You fathers, again, must not goad your children into resentment. . . ." Paul is clear at this point. There's a commandment for the children to obey, but there's a commandment for parents, too. Parents must be worthy of respect and honor. If a mother and father do not learn how to control their anger, what right do they have to ask their children to control theirs?

If the first ingredient of the command is discipline, the second is direction. Parents are to direct their children's actions, not by dogging them, not by deflating them, not by demeaning them, but by lovingly, firmly directing them and disciplining them.

Every child learns three things from his parents. He

learns his concept of reality (what the world is like, what the universe is like, the laws of life). He learns his concept of God. And he learns his concept of himself. When parents overcorrect and goad their children into resentment, the last two concepts are gravely distorted. When parents are overstrict, harsh and unbending, their discipline becomes destructive and damaging. What happens if a child never gets approval, is always cut down, nagged and criticized? Often these children, even those from the most religious homes, get the wrong concept of God and themselves.

The Skylight

Years ago a great Christian psychiatrist said, "Whenever you see over-conscientious parents, look around for emotional wreckage." And may I add for spiritual wreckage too. Mother and Dad are the skylight through which a child gets his or her first look at God. Mother and Father are also the mirror in which a child sees a reflection of himself or herself. The little child's selfhood is determined by the reflected appraisal of the adults and the parents who surround him. Parents are to discipline and direct but not to destroy.

The third ingredient of the commandment, after discipline and direction, is devotion. "Bring them up," says Paul, "in the training and instruction of the Lord." This is as much a part of the fifth commandment as it is for the child to obey the parents and the parents not to goad the child into resentment. Paul is telling us that God's plan includes a family devotional life.

Some years ago the University of Chicago asked a number of graduate students, "Where did you get your major ideas about morals and religion?" The chief answer was this simple sentence, "Through my family's mealtime conversation."

Do you have family worship at your house? That's a

part of the commandment, too. This part of the commandment is just as divinely inspired as the command for the child to obey his parents and parents to respect the essential selfhood of the child. Parents, are you obeying this part of the commandment?

A Command And A Promise

*   John Ruskin said the history of the world is not the record of its great wars but the history of its households. No nation can be lifted higher than its homes. No nation can survive unless its homes are strong. God has given us a command and a promise. It's a command that children obey and honor their parents, and that parents be the kind of persons that children can respect and honor. It's a command that parents instruct and bring their children up in the teachings and way of the Lord. And it's a command that both parents and children learn obedience and love, honor and respect, not just once a week in church but every day of the week in the greatest temple of all, the home.

The fifth commandment was broadened in the New Testament, but it has never been repealed. It is still one of God's eternal commands. Children obey your parents in the Lord. Parents don't overcorrect your children; bring them up in the discipline and instruction of the Lord. If we fail to keep this commandment we make ourselves and our decendants vulnerable to heartbreak. If we keep this commandment succeeding generations will thank us.

8

Tampering With God's Most Sacred Gift

You shall not murder (Exodus 20:13).

You have heard that it was said to the people long ago, "Do not murder, and anyone who murders will be subject to judgment." But I tell you that anyone who is angry with his brother will be subject to judgment. Again, anyone who says to his brother, "Raca"* is answerable to the Sanhedrin. But anyone who says, "You fool!" will be in danger of the fire of hell. . . .

You have heard that it was said, "Love your neighbor and hate your enemy." But I tell you: Love your enemies and pray for those who persecute you, that you may be sons of your Father in Heaven (from Jesus' Sermon on the Mount, Matthew 5:21-22, 43-45)

*an Aramaic term of contempt

The sixth commandment lifts human life to the highest possible level because it recognizes that life is sacred. Life is God's gift, and we must not tamper with it. No person can restore life once it has ended. To kill is a wrong which once done cannot be undone. The finality of the taking of a human life has caused every civilization, no matter how seemingly primitive, to surround it with prohibitions and regulations.

Often after a murder or a fatal accident a grieving

parent or a loved one would tell me when I was a pastor, "I don't care about prosecuting the case. I'm not interested in that. Nothing can bring him back."

Shakespeare's Othello is haunted by one thought after he decides to kill the woman he loves: I can put out a light, and I can restore that light once it's put out, but the light of life once put out can never be restored.

Murder And Modern Complexities

Now we won't belabor the obvious. Murder is murder. But the complexities of modern life have created some much more subtle problems. We will explore a few of them in this chapter.

This commandment deals with the principle of physical life and death. The basic issue is simply this: God alone has sovereignty over life. In 1 Samuel 2:6, where Hannah is praising God for the birth of her son Samuel, she poetically states a great truth: "The Lord brings death and makes alive." God alone is the creator of life. Likewise God alone has the right to determine the end of life.

Now let's not confuse this commandment with sentimentality regarding animal life, as did Albert Schweitzer. I'm not criticizing his philosophy, though it is more Hindu than biblical. Don't misunderstand me. Almost no other book in all the world calls for more mercy to be given to animals, especially suffering animals, than the Bible. And the Bible's humane commands for protecting animals were given at a time when kindness to animals wasn't dreamed of by most people, not even in the most advanced civilizations of the day. Nevertheless the sixth commandment is not to be combined with an over-active reverence for life. That may be a noble philosophy, but having lived in India I know that it doesn't work in practical experience. The dreadful condition of most of its so-called "sacred cows" is witness to this fact.

I'll never forget when Prime Minister Nehru came to our little town of Bidar in India. One of his remarks was, "As I drove into your community I noticed the pathetic condition of the cattle in this district. My, how I wish we could treat our cattle in India, where we profess to worship them, in some small degree as well as they do in the United States of America, where they do not claim to worship them." When we fail to see the hierarchy of life, we miss a great biblical principle. The sixth commandment refers to human life; it does not abolish the sovereignty that man has over animal life. This jurisdiction was plainly given by the Lord God himself in Genesis 1:28 and especially in Genesis 9:1-6.

Presuming To Be Like God

So what is this sixth commandment really saying? The actual commandment is this: "You shall not murder." It's striking that the verb used here for "to murder" is never used in the Bible for things like killing an opponent in war or for executing someone who has been condemned to death. Murder is the ending of a human life, a prerogative which belongs only to God. If we take this right into our own hands we presume to be like God, which is one of humanity's oldest temptations, dating back to the serpent's hiss in Genesis 3:5, "You will be like God."

As always, to fully understand this sixth commandment we must reaffirm the first two commandments, which tell us that only God will be God of our lives. History is replete with illustrations, from ancient Rome to Hitler, that only when God is truly God is mankind truly human. Only when God counts for everything does man amount to anything. We must maintain this important hierarchy.

With this in mind let us see how the sixth commandment guides us amid some of the complexities of modern life. The commandment forbids killing a person directly, as when Cain murdered Abel, or indirectly, as when David killed Uriah by ordering someone else to do it.

The Sixth Commandment And Suicide

But what about suicide? Surely one of our basic human rights is to say with Hamlet, "To be or not to be?" But suicide isn't a basic human right. As in any other murder it involves the taking of authority that belongs only to God. If God does not allow us to murder another human, he certainly does not allow us to murder ourselves. Some ask, "How can suicide be wrong when my life belongs to me?" The problem with this argument is that, according to the Scriptures, it doesn't. Your life belongs to God. Paul says, "You are not your own. . ." (1 Corinthians 6:19). Taking your life is a privilege which only belongs to God and no Christian can do it. Suicide *is* a form of murder.

You may wonder why I am spending time on this subject. Suicide must be addressed honestly because for the last several years it has surpassed traffic accidents as the chief cause of death among young people. People need to know that suicide is murder because it involves a person giving himself or herself the right to be an exceptional case and to take exceptional power into his or her own hands.

I'm not condemning those who commit suicide. God alone is their judge. I think of that plaintive verse, Psalm 73:26, where the Psalmist cries out in deep distress, "My flesh and my heart may fail." And sometimes they do fail. God alone can be our judge. In my own mind I believe that several people I know who have committed suicide are with the Lord. I think some people are driven to such an extent by certain mental difficul-

ties and emotional problems that their hearts and
minds literally do fail them. They are then no longer
capable of making a responsible decision. But I must
say that on a scriptural basis, suicide is definitely a
form of murder and is not an option open to a responsible Christian.

What About War?

Another perennial question relating to the sixth
commandment is, "Is war wrong?" There are two answers to this question, and you may quote saints and
scholars of equal worth on either side. Some say Christ
addresses this when he tells us we must love our enemies and not resist evil with force (Matthew 5:39-45),
and that those who draw the sword will die by it (Matthew 26:52). War is a terrible killer, not only of com-
batants but also of millions of innocents. War, say some
people, is always wrong.

But equally scholarly and saintly Christians say
war is not always wrong. They argue that when evil
men and evil systems become aggressive, they have to
be stopped. Just as the judge has a right to condemn the
murderer or the policeman has the right to shoot an
armed criminal breaking into a home, so a government
has the right to become an instrument of justice to stop
evil men and nations.

Now this ancient Christian dilemma is something
you have to settle in your own heart, between you and
God. No one else can settle it for you. It is not an easy
question.

However one thing is sure—Christ never gives us,
under any circumstances, the right to hate our enemies.
If you opt for war it must be done in agony of spirit and
only as a last resort. It must be done regretfully, repen-
tantly and realizing that it is not a second best decision
but a ghastly last choice. A Christian will not indulge

hatred, a revengeful spirit, bitterness or gloating over a fallen enemy. A Christian will instead show only love, forgiveness and mercy, even in the midst of war.

But our modern world raises questions about even more complex forms of modern murder. For example, in 1973 the Supreme Court's infamous *Roe v. Wade* ruling stated that the law doesn't regard abortion as murder. Is abortion murder? The Supreme Court has forced the Church to make a Christian decision in this matter.

Now let's not confuse the issue of abortion with that of birth control. As a Protestant I believe that it is right to plan our families and space children properly for the health of the mother. Birth control might be more properly termed "conception control." It prevents the possible beginning of human life. I think that in today's world responsible family planning is a Christian obligation. But such birth control should not be confused with abortion. Abortion is the destruction of human life after it has begun.

Truly Human
The only really important question here is: What lives inside the mother after the time of conception? Is it truly a human life? Or is it, as the proponents of liberal abortion claim, just a part of the mother? If so its removal should be as simple as taking out an appendix or a gall bladder. If we can believe this, the only thing that deserves consideration is the mother's health or some social standard of well-being. But if the growing object within the mother is a human being then, from a Christian standpoint, the sixth commandment applies, and that being deserves protection as a sacred human life.

We can't discuss all the arguments pro and con here. But I believe with all my heart that the medical evidence—the intricate studies, even photographs of the

fetus practically from the time of conception onward—
means that we must honestly say that the fetus is alive,
is a human being and, even within only a few weeks, is
remarkably complete. He is more than just a potential
human being; he is a human being with vast potential.
The only change that takes place when he is born is in
his external life support system. His human beingness
is not acquired by development; later development is
just a growing expression of his innate humanity. I
believe that abortion is definitely the taking of human
life.

To me it is best to candidly acknowledge that abortion is the killing of a human life. Then we can face the
questions raised by any very extreme cases where abortion may be a last choice. Very frankly, once in my life
I approved of an abortion. Only once. In that case the
young woman's father was the father of her child.
Therefore I'm not saying that in absolutely no case
should abortion be considered. I'm simply saying that
we should realize it's a very serious matter and a sober-
ing responsibility. Let's make sure, under God, that the
proposed good far outweighs the commandment not to
kill. In any such case one commandment may have to
be superceded rather than broken.

What's Next?

When we enter this difficult area of abortion we're
close to some very great dangers. The moment a nation
becomes lax at one such point, what is the next step?
Why not legalize the killing of old people who are no
longer useful? Why not kill mentally defective babies at
birth? You may think I'm exaggerating. However less
than six months after England passed a permissive
abortion law, a law was introduced into the parliament
to legalize mercy killing. It was barely defeated.

We must be careful. We live in a complex world

where there are many ways to murder others and ourselves, and we must take them very seriously. Some people dig their graves with their knives and forks, literally murdering themselves by overeating. Others allow bad habits to injure their bodies. Someone once asked me why I never preach against smoking. I said, "Why should I waste my time when the American Cancer Society does such a good job of it?" The medical evidence is all there. The same applies to alcohol or drug abuse or any bad habit that dissipates the body and makes it less effective for Christ.

Can we murder by carelessness? By reckless driving? Yes. We can murder when we do anything for personal gain or pleasure that puts someone else's life in danger. Examples of this are the engineer who knowingly designs a faulty roof for a house to make more money or the person who drives a car after drinking. Children can murder their parents by sending them to a premature grave by disobedience, ingratitude, neglect, rebellion and cruelty. These are all forms of murder. Today more than ever we must think about the vast implications of the sixth commandment.

Jesus Elevates The Commandment
In the New Testament Jesus restated this ancient commandment in his Sermon on the Mount and in no way nullified it. Instead he raised it to a much higher level, probing deep into our hearts. The passage quoted at the beginning of this chapter was probably not popular with his listeners. The Jews lived under the heels of the cruel Romans. Although they hadn't fought those Romans since the time of the Maccabees, they still hated them. No doubt many Jews imagined all sorts of delicious tortures and painful deaths for the Romans. But Jesus struck deep into their hearts, just as he delves into our hearts. The old commandment pro-

hibited only the outward blows which would kill. Jesus
expanded it to include the inward things such as resentment, bad feelings, passions and insults which could
lead later to physical blows. In other words, Jesus
warns us against anger.

We consider anger an unavoidable human frailty.
Jesus is not forbidding proper anger, which is a part of
human life. Jesus himself got angry at the right time,
at the right place, about the right things. A lot of Christians need to learn how to get angry like that. However,
Jesus did condemn personal anger, that out-of-control
type of resentful emotion. Jesus says the only difference
between murder and anger or insult and hate is in degree. And isn't that often the order in which killing occurs? First comes seething resentment, insult, hatred
and finally murder.

Forgiveness And Reconciliation

Some of us murder slowly in our own homes with
our uncontrollable temper and insulting remarks which
harden into resentment. As Jesus gives us a broader
view of this sixth commandment he makes us responsible for taking the initiative to love someone who
is unloving and even unloveable. "You," Jesus says in
effect, "as my disciple, must make the first move toward
forgiveness and reconciliation."

Jesus realized anyone who hurt, insulted or hated
him was a person in deep spiritual need—in need of his
love. We do just the opposite. We become angry when
we've been hurt because we're concerned about ourselves. But Jesus cared about the other person, even
when it cost him his life. Jesus told us, "Therefore, if
you are offering your gift at the altar and there remember that your brother has something against you, leave
your gift there in front of the altar. First go and be rec-
onciled to your brother; then come and offer your gift"

(Matthew 5:23-24). Jesus knew how easily we break the sixth commandment.

"Don't kill your enemy," is what Jesus is saying. "Love him to death instead. Kill your enemy by loving him until he dies as an enemy and is reborn as a friend." That's not easy, but Jesus never said it would be. It may cost you your prestige, your name and your power. It would be impossible, except that as we share in the spirit of Ephesians 4:32 which tells us, "Be kind and compassionate to one another, forgiving each other, *just as in Christ God forgave you.*"

9

Sanctity In A Sex-Saturated Society

You shall not commit adultery (Exodus 20:14).

The body is not meant for sexual immorality, but for the Lord, and the Lord for the body. By his power God raised the Lord from the dead, and he will raise us also. Do you not know that your bodies are members of Christ himself? Shall I then take the members of Christ and unite them with a prostitute? Never! Do you not know that he who unites himself with a prostitute is one with her in body? For it is said, "The two will become one flesh." But he who unites himself with the Lord is one with him in spirit.

Flee from sexual immorality. All other sins a man commits are outside his body, but he who sins sexually sins against his own body. Do you not know that your body is a temple of the Holy Spirit, who is in you, whom you have received from God? You are not your own; you were bought at a price. Therefore honor God with your body (1 Corinthians 6:13-20).

A discussion of the seventh of the Ten Commandments reminds many of us of those summer youth camp lectures on sex with titles like "Watch Out—You're Playing with Fire," "Backseat Christianity," or "How Far Can We Go?" Or you may remember admonitions you heard as a teenager, such as, "never kiss longer than three seconds at one time," "always make sure you double date, especially with a missionary's son" or maybe "keep your hands where they belong."

As adult Christians, however, we need to give God a fresh opportunity to address us on this subject.

The seventh commandment is perhaps the most unpopular of all the Ten Commandments, and the one under the heaviest fire today. Some of the other commandments are laughed at or ignored, but the seventh commandment is under a direct philosophical and theological assault by almost every force in modern society including, believe it or not, some segments within the Church itself. We are living in a sex-saturated society, a society in which the media tells us in a thousand and one ways, "Thou *shall* lust, in thought, word and deed."

Sex And Cereal

Just think for a moment of the alarming attack on the authority of the seventh commandment mounted by this adulterous generation. The first is *advertising*. Sex is used to sell absolutely everything imaginable and some things that are utterly unimaginable. Some of the most unromantic things one could think of, including automobiles, hamburgers, tires, batteries, cigarettes, cereal and many other commodities, are being promoted by using sexual ads.

The second attack is *amusement*. We have now reached that stage described in Romans 1:32 where Paul, after describing many sexual sins, says, "they not only continue to do these very things but also approve of those who practice them." Our comedians, television shows, movies and novels ridicule or depict as abnormal the Christian faith's teachings concerning sexual purity and sanctity. Marriage, chastity, commitment and self-control are derided and dismissed.

Outright lust is not just big business, it is practically

the biggest business, for it promotes all other businesses through advertisement and amusement.

Fords And Freedom
Another attack on the seventh commandment comes from the *automobile*. (I use it here to symbolize the many modern forms of transportation that have given Americans a freedom hitherto unknown in relationships between men and women.) It can short-circuit time, place, distance and moral restraints. Let's face it. The automobile is a compact mobile home and, if so desired, a portable bedroom. The automobile is an often overlooked accomplice in the drastic attack on the sanctity of sex because it gives speedy opportunity for easy access to the sexual temptations we face.

Add *alcohol* to our list (notice these are all beginning with the letter "A"). A few years ago I wouldn't have included this because I would have thought it entirely unnecessary. But I'm increasingly astounded at the number of evangelical Christians who see nothing wrong with drinking. Liquor is an increasing threat, especially to our young people, even evangelical young people. The terrific pressure to take that first seemingly innocent social drink becomes greater all the time.

Any fool can see the intimate, intricate connection between alcohol and sex. It is perhaps the only drug on the market that works two ways at the same time: It inflames desire and weakens willpower simultaneously. It makes people eager to say "yes" and weakens their ability to say "no." This is not always true, but the person who drinks is at greater risk of yielding to sexual temptation (which can be difficult enough to avoid when sober). The alcohol problem is intricately connected with our society's assault on Christian morality.

We can add another "A," *anarchy* in morals. I know

a lot of people think I exaggerate. I was always accused by some of being a dirty old man in my preaching—I always talked about "it" too much. But those people didn't sit with me hour after hour in my counseling room and hear what I heard. Higher statistics on immoral behavior can easily be proved. However, we are talking about something even more serious. Sexual sin has always existed, but for the first time a rational, logically presented philosophy of immorality or amorality has emerged.

It began with the playboy philosophy that developed in the 1960s, which can be summarized like this: "Sex is a function of the body, a drive we share with animals, like eating, drinking and sleeping. It is a physical demand that must be satisfied. If we don't satisfy it, the repression will cause all sorts of neuroses and psychoses. Let's forget the prudery that makes us hide from it. Throw away those inhibitions. Find a like-minded partner and let yourself go." This is basically the modern philosophy of immorality or amorality that is battling the biblical perspective on sex.

Relationships Instead of Commitment

may remember that in the famous 1970 movie "Love Story," Jennifer and Oliver changed the word "marriage" to "agreement," thus ushering in a new emphasis on relationship instead of commitment. One writer has summarized this revolution in morals as: "The key to the new morality is the widespread belief that a man and a woman who have established 'a meaningful relationship' have a moral right to sleep together. If two people are in love there's nothing wrong with their sleeping together provided no one is hurt by it." This describes a philosophy of morality that has developed in the last 20 to 30 years. It is something far more dangerous than simply statistics of immoral behavior. Our society is making a concerted, philosophical attempt to defend immorality. This is what I mean by anarchy in morality.

Another "A" word we must add to our list of attacks on the seventh commandment is perhaps the most amazing of them all: *accommodation*. This new morality is actually being accommodated by some people in the church. It is astounding to hear certain well-known religious leaders concede that there are exceptions to the Christian view that sexual relations outside marriage are always wrong. One of them explains it this way: "Sex may be an act of charity which proclaims the glory of God, or may be an act of healing. Where there is healing there is Christ, whatever the church may have to say about fornication." Another supposed Christian publication has gone on record as saying, "It must be accepted as a fact that light-hearted and loving casual contact can be known without profound damage or moral degeneracy to either partner."

Evangelical Erosion

The final assault doesn't begin with an "A," but with an "E" for evangelical. That may startle you. However, evangelicals are being poisoned by this onslaught on the seventh commandment and on the high standard of Christian sexual ethics. Even evangelicals are giving in to a sure, slow erosion of high standards of sexual behavior. I repeat, it's not just the fact that statistics show a higher rate of immoral behavior that is disturbing. When I was young, some of the best of us jumped the moral fences. But the point is, we had fences. We knew exactly where those fences were, even though we did not always stay within them. The problem now, however, is that evangelicals themselves are removing the fences. Do you know where the fences are? Or are you conforming to today's sex-saturated society with its all-out attack on the seventh commandment?

The March, 18, 1988 issue of *Christianity Today* described a shocking survey commissioned by the Josh McDowell Ministry. It revealed that 65 percent of teenagers attending fundamental, evangelical churches have had some type of sexual contact by age 18, and 43 percent have experienced sexual intercourse by that age. Even at the tender age of 13, 20 percent of the church-going youth surveyed had engaged in some sexual experimentation. Those figures are only 10 to 15 percentage points behind the latest general youth population surveys.

"Number One" Barrier

The study found that the "number one" barrier to youthful sexual activity was being "born again and committed to the Bible." Those who said they were born again were less than half as likely to be sexually active.

However, churches cannot assume that religious training and experience will automatically protect their young people from premature sexual involvement. Jim Watkins, editorial director of teen ministries for the Wesleyan Church, one of the eight denominations included in the survey, said the study "will help us convince people this is a problem within the holiness denominations as well as the high school and junior highs."

Concerning where young people get their information about sex, 57 percent of those surveyed said at least "some" came from movies, while 73 percent said they got "a little" or "none" of their sexual information from the church. Obviously we are not giving our youth enough guidance in this important and confusing area of their lives. We cannot assume that our children will wait until marriage to have sex simply because they are growing up in a Christian home. We must teach them where the moral fences are and why they exist. But we cannot guide our youth if we ourselves are accommodating our culture's immoral modern philosophy.

As Christians we can talk frankly and positively about sexual issues. God begins his Word by telling us that he approves of sex. That may surprise some of us. But Genesis 2:24 says that a man leaves his father and his mother and is joined to his wife in such a way that the two become one person. Even before Adam had a chance to kiss Eve hello, God put his approval on the world's first honeymoon. John Milton captures this beautifully in his famous work, *Paradise Lost*.

"So pass'd they naked on, nor shunn'd the sight
Of God or Angel, for they thought no ill:
So hand in hand they pass'd, the loveliest pair
That ever since in love's embraces met"
(Book IV, lines 319-322).

And in spite of the fall of man, the Old Testament contains some fantastic love stories that make a lot of our modern ideas of romance sound like pablum out of a cheap paperback novel.

We read about Rebecca traveling across the desert and fields to greet Isaac, her new love. We read how Jacob worked 14 years for his father-in-law to win the hand of his sweetheart, Rachel. 1 Samuel tells a beautiful story of how Hannah and Elkanah faced the challenge of a childless marriage in prayer and in praise.

Explicit And Eloquent

Interestingly, the Old and New Testaments are both explicit and eloquent when they discuss sex. The New Testament relates the word sex to the body. Some misguided prudes may consider "body" a dirty word, but the New Testament does not. Paul explains in 1 Corinthians 6:18-20 that God considers our bodies important because they are the home of the Holy Spirit. Since our bodies are sacred, they are to be offered as living sacrifices, which Paul calls a reasonable and a spiritual service (Romans 12:1).

But if God is so delighted about sex, many people wonder, and approves of our bodies, why did he give us the seventh commandment? The question misses the point. We have the seventh commandment precisely because sex is God's idea. "You shall not commit adultery" is God's response to our blatant abuse of this great gift of sexuality. He recoils at the thought of a man leaving his home in the middle of the night and going to sleep with his neighbor's wife. He is disgusted by the woman who sells her body and the men who pay her. He's angry with the rebellious teenager who demands to indulge unbridled passion. The seventh commandment is God's response to such selfish desires for gratification. Sex is perhaps the highest form of human ecstasy that God has given to us. But it can be enjoyed only within God's approved form for intimate sexual expression—marriage. Ironically, when we break the seventh commandment by having sex outside of marriage we expose ourselves to a legion of mental and physical consequences that can ultimately rob us of any sexual enjoyment.

Jesus Included Thoughts

When Jesus restated the seventh commandment in Matthew 5:27-28 he broadened it, just as He had the sixth, to include thoughts: "You have heard that it was said, 'Do not commit adultery.' But I tell you that anyone who looks at a woman lustfully has already committed adultery with her in his heart." The Christian standard is simply this: you shall not lust in thought, word or deed. Faithfulness to your marriage partner is mandatory. This is the Christian ethic of sex. You may not agree with it. The world certainly doesn't like it. You may choose to reject it. But as a Christian you may not repeal it or revise it.

Still some say, "Wait a minute. Why is God so strong on this commandment? Why does he allow full sexual expression only in one form—namely, within marriage?" Simply because he knows that human beings are not capable of emotionally handling a number of intimate relationships. What God is really asking us to do is respect individuals. The sin of adultery is not merely the physical act. It is that act's degrading effect on human character. Adultery is doing the right thing in a wrong relationship, a relationship outside that which is clearly specified by the Word of God.

Sex is the most tangible way we can give our love to someone. It involves much more than our bodies. During sex we give our most precious, private feelings. We offer the essence of our personality. When we engage in sex with someone other than our mates we trample upon velvet feelings and sensitivities. The adulterer is misusing another person.

Wiping Our Feet On Love

The word "adultery" comes from the Hebrew word which means adulteration. The term was first used when the Israelites were worshiping idols, thereby adulterating pure Jehovah worship with impure gods and goddesses. They had defaced what was originally chaste and clean. That's what adultery is. It's when we use extramarital relationships to wipe our feet on the pure love that God has given us. When we understand this deeper meaning of adultery, fidelity in marriage makes sense; anything else seems unreasonable.

But what does the seventh commandment say to those who are not married? The New Testament almost always uses the term "adultery" to refer to a married person. It uses a different word for sex between two unmarried persons: "fornication." But the New Testament restatement of the seventh commandment is just as strict, just as straightforward, regarding fornication as it is adultery. The concern for the feelings of someone else, the concern for the fidelity of pledged love is the same. Fornication refers to premarital relations instead of extramarital relations, but the message is exactly the same—there is no difference, scripturally speaking, between fornication and adultery.

However, many unmarried people don't buy this. They say, "What's wrong with the modern philosophy? We're in love. We have a meaningful relationship. Why can't we have an intimate sexual relationship?"

Dark Corners

To begin with, conduct like extramarital or premarital affairs has to be done in secret, since not even our semi-civilized society approves of it. Those who have such affairs are forced to drag something that God meant to be holy, joyful and wonderful into a lot of dark corners. The secrecy of furtive moments in the backseats of automobiles and clandestine meetings in forbidden rooms brings fear and a sense of guilt. The nagging anxiety is that someone might find out.

Proverbs 28:1 says, "The wicked man flees though no one pursues." To live in this kind of fear is wretchedness. Such a situation affects your energy and your whole outlook on life. It may even affect the love that you are trying to preserve in the intimacy of those relationships. In my counseling experience I've seen secrecy and guilt ravage a couple's self-respect and destroy the very love they think they are expressing to one another.

But why do people who engage in fornication and adultery feel this sense of guilt? They may excuse their behavior, may justify it and may do some fancy philosophical sidestepping, but their conscience will eventually tackle them and throw them for a loss. Is this simply because they heard stern warnings about extramarital sex from their parents or some church? No. I believe it is because this commandment, like every commandment, is written deeply into the fiber of our being.

I remember a young lady once told me, "It's all right if I get by with it." But a few months later she was back in my office, in tears.

I said, "What's wrong? I thought you said it was all right if you could get by with it. Did someone find out?"

"Oh, no," she said, "not at all. But I know. And I discovered nothing is worse than living with myself when I can't respect myself. By giving myself to someone I've really lost respect for, I've literally been living in hell."

Written In Our Personality
The modern philosophy says "throw away your inhibitions; find a partner who thinks the same, let yourself go and have a lot of fun." But why doesn't this work? Is it because thousands of years ago Moses claimed God gave him a command and wrote "Thou shalt not commit adultery" on tablets of stone? No. The reason is because the commandments come out of the Holy nature and character of God. Since you and I are made in the image of God, this command is written into our human personality. I believe it is written into us physically, mentally, emotionally and spiritually.

For example, a University of Tennessee study among young women found: "There seems to be a direct correlation between illicit sexual behavior and serious emotional problems." University after university finds that the people who regularly seek counseling are the ones who are violating the seventh commandment. Kirkendahl at the University of Oregon studied young men and found that those who engage in premarital relationships make poor marital risks. They are unable to properly relate to all persons, both men and women.

The seventh commandment also meets our human needs in a physical way. God's plan of sexual morality can prevent a host of health problems. The most notorious of these is the recently-emerged Acquired Immune Deficiency Syndrome, but venereal diseases have been wreaking havoc on humanity for centuries. Even ardent advocates of "safe sex" acknowledge that the only 100 percent reliable protection against AIDS and other sexually transmitted diseases is a mutually monogamous relationship.

In addition to sexually transmitted diseases, unwanted pregnancy is always a possibility, no matter what type of birth control a couple uses. Unplanned parenthood can be a problem within a marriage but is always an unspeakable tragedy outside of it. Unmarried parents find their only options are abortion, adoption or raising the child under difficult circumstances—"solutions" that lead to years of mental anguish.

These serious consequences of illicit sexual behavior prove that God's plan is meant to ensure our happiness and well being.

Agony And Ecstasy

Many people discover the paradox of agony and ecstasy regarding sexual relationships outside of marriage. Seconds of gratification and thrill are followed by agonizing minutes on the way home when silence fills the guilt-ridden car. They grit their teeth as they enter the door to their home and say "never again," only to helplessly repeat those words a few weekends later. They may cry, "Oh, God help me," as they sob themselves to sleep.

Christ is compassionate about our weaknesses. He was especially understanding toward people who couldn't handle their sex drives. He forgave the woman at the well (John 4) and the adulteress in John 8. Nevertheless he sent them away saying, "Go and sin no more." Sexual relations outside of marriage are no worse than lying and murder and stealing. Like other sins, adultery and fornication *can* be forgiven if we are sincerely interested in letting Christ change us. To do this we must begin with our minds.

Jesus says that sexual self-control is a matter of attitude. If you expose yourself to sexually-explicit magazines, novels, movies or TV shows you are not helping yourself resist temptation. If you go to see the latest skin flick and think you will keep your mind on the Pepsi-Cola and pizza afterward, you are entirely wrong. Sexual morality begins with your attitude.

Transformed Not Conformed

Paul writes in Romans 12:2, ". . .be transformed by the renewing of your mind." I think a couple should decide on a standard of behavior together and on their knees make a commitment to that standard. They must allow absolutely no leeway for rationalizing the lowering of that standard, because the moment they begin to lower that standard I can tell you exactly what they will end up doing.

Why do I speak so urgently in a book that will be read primarily by Christian believers? Because as long ago as 1970 a survey found three out of every four women college students lost their virginity. Gallup polls showed a 24 percent increase in the 1970s in premarital relations for students in evangelical denominational colleges. The statistics cited earlier in this chapter show that even church-going youth are not saving sex for marriage. The world is laughing at us, and God is weeping over us as we trample the seventh commandment.

Now, let's face it, nothing I say here will make any

difference in your life unless you want it to. But if you want to avoid sexual temptations, every resource of the Spirit is yours.

10

Why There's No Free Lunch

You shall not steal (Exodus 20:15).

Do you not know that your body is a temple of the Holy Spirit, who is in you, whom you have received from God? You are not your own; you were bought at a price (1 Corinthians 6:19-20).

Of all the commandments in the Bible, this one seems to be the most clear-cut. On the surface it looks very simple. You would think it needs no explanation at all. To steal means the same thing today as it did then: the taking of something which belongs to someone else.

This commandment is probably the most universal of all of the laws in the world. For example, some primitive cultures had no taboo against immorality as long as neither party was married. But if one of the parties were married adultery was strictly forbidden, not because it was immoral but because it was considered a form of theft, "stealing" another person's spouse. Often the matter was settled by the offender's simply paying the husband in cows or goats or money the sum the husband originally paid for the wife.

Just as the sixth commandment (you shall not murder) safeguards life and the seventh commandment (you shall not commit adultery) safeguards love and the family, this eighth commandment safeguards property.

It forbids theft, the taking or keeping of something that belongs to someone else.

But the New Testament and the church have always given this eighth commandment much deeper meaning. We must understand some of that meaning if this commandment is to have Christian relevance for us in our modern, complex society.

But let's begin our study at the Old Testament level. Even at that level, this commandment is desperately needed today.

Widely Broken Commandment

The eighth commandment has always been widely broken. The latest crime statistics always shock us. Thievery and hold-ups, breaking and entering, all forms of old-fashioned stealing, are fed by our nation's drug problem as addicts struggle to maintain exorbitantly expensive habits. White collar crime, shenanigans in high finance and cheating on government taxes prove this sin is not confined to the lower income levels. The cost of crime is now in the billions of dollars a year. The eighth commandment is being broken many times each second as you read this chapter.

Therefore, let's not even suggest that the commandment is outdated. It isn't. "But wait a minute," you say, "this doesn't apply to us. We're Christians. We don't need to be lectured about thievery." However, the New Testament is not as naive as we are. It is filled with warnings to Christians.

Outright stealing is far more common among church members and professing Christians than we like to admit. I find it an increasingly common sin that is confessed at the altar or in the counseling room. The larceny may involve anything, whether fountain pens and cosmetics at the drugstore, groceries at the supermarket, a roommate's money, tools at the filling station or a book from the library.

Somehow, if God were to fly over our churches in a great spy plane photographing our hearts, those pictures might be as shocking as when the U2 plane flew over Cuba and discovered the secret missiles. In fact if we were to expose our hearts to the Holy Spirit, perhaps every one of us would discover some place in our lives where we need to acknowledge and make right a violation of this commandment. And if you think that some subtle, clever, sophisticated reinterpretation of this basic commandment allows a hidden dishonesty in your life, then you will be disappointed in the Scriptures. Paul puts it very bluntly: "put off your old self. . . ." followed by a list of things to put off, including "He who has been stealing must steal no longer. . ." (Ephesians 4:22, 28). God cannot and will not condone any form of stealing.

Paul also writes in 1 Corinthians 6:9-10, "Do you not know that the wicked will not inherit the kingdom of God? Do not be deceived: Neither the sexually immoral nor idolaters. . .nor thieves nor the greedy. . .nor swindlers will inherit the kingdom of God." Notice that two types of sinners who break the eighth commandment are included in this long list of transgressors: thieves and swindlers.

Cheating And Restitution

The Scriptures also tell us that restitution is sometimes necessary. Zacchaeus, the notorious tax collector, promised to pay back four times the amount that he had cheated anyone. After he made that vow, Jesus, knowing the true repentance in Zacchaeus' heart, joyfully said, "Today salvation has come to this house. . .(see Luke 19:1-10). Likewise, we may never really know the joy of realizing that our sins are forgiven unless we do confess and right some wrongs in this area of our lives.

Now let's examine the eighth commandment on another level. The Bible is filled with examples of various ways this commandment can be broken. We need to study these to discover the basic principle behind the eighth commandment. It applies to much more than mere burglary. A lot of theft is not direct but indirect. Some of us keep the letter of the law but violate the spirit of the commandment. Human ingenuity can work overtime to produce subtle evasions of the eighth commandment.

Consider Jacob and Esau, for example (see Genesis 25:24-34 and 27:1-40). Esau was working outside on a blistering summer day, perhaps hunting wild game as he was fond of doing. He returned late in the afternoon, worn out, desperate for something to eat and a cold drink. His twin brother Jacob, the deceiver, the crooked one, knew Esau's weaknesses. Jacob deliberately prepared a delicious meal of stew with a cold drink. Knowing Esau's hasty and passionate nature, Jacob refused to give Esau any food or drink until Esau, the firstborn, gave Jacob his birthright. In his famished condition, Esau sold his birthright to Jacob for the meal. Later Jacob deceived his elderly, blind father Isaac into giving him Esau's blessing as well. The Bible says that Jacob "took" Esau's birthright and blessing (Genesis 27:35-36). It doesn't say that Esau sold them but that Jacob stole them through trickery and deceit. I believe there is a lesson here for us.

Making The Hard Bargain

Some Christians think they are best known in their communities for their strong profession of faith, but they are not. They are best known as the ones who drive the hardest bargains, who make the clever business deals, who exploit an advantage whenever possible. This is the person about whom people say, "I wouldn't do business with him or her because in every deal you have a strange way of coming out on the short end of things."

Is deceiving, making the sharp, hard bargain stealing in the biblical sense of the word? To answer that question let's look at another example. Did Jesus drive the merchants out of the temple because they were selling birds and other things in there? No. Birds and animals were always sold in the temple because devout Jews needed them to make sacrifices. But these merchants were taking advantage of the situation to profit from poor people. They drove the poor into debt by charging unfair prices. Jesus said they had turned God's house into a "den of robbers" (Matthew 21:13). So Jesus considered taking unfair advantage an act of thievery.

A Deeper Pit

The Bible is clear. The Old Testament prophets loudly declare God's judgment upon anyone who takes advantage of someone in need. From the biblical standpoint, to overcharge, to undersell or to deceive is to steal. Even in Dante's description of hell the swindler is in a much deeper pit than the armed robber or the thief.

Then there's that fine art of stealing known by the fancy name "income tax evasion." It may be the most serious kind of theft in the United States today because of the huge number of people involved. As our legislators try to balance our massive national debt, they frequently point out that eliminating tax dodging would go a long way to helping them reach their elusive goal. Are we scrupulously honest at this point? Stealing is stealing, whether it be from an individual, a government, a corporation or the nation as a whole.

Now I believe that we must also label as stealing the

taking of money or anything of value as a result of gambling. I base this belief on the principle behind the eighth commandment: stealing is basically trying to get something for nothing. It's trying to gain something at the expense of another person. It is not just a violation of the sacredness of property, but a violation of the principle of stewardship, the trusteeship of possessions. Ultimately, any money won through gambling comes out of another person's pocket. Often that other person is poor and can ill afford it or is a compulsive gambler in the grip of a terrible addiction.

Do you realize the extent of the sin of gambling in our country? Betting on horses and dog races at tracks in our country is a multi-billion dollar business. Each week millions of dollars change hands in betting on professional sports. These are just two examples of the many forms gambling takes in our society. Is there a connection between gambling and actual stealing? The American Insurance Institute has estimated that up to 40 percent of white collar crime, such as embezzlement, can be traced to compulsive gambling.

FBI crime reports have shown that states that allow gambling have a much higher crime rate than non-gambling states. The idea that a nation can raise money by gambling is a myth. For every dollar generated by gambling several dollars are required in higher police, court, penitentiary and relief costs. Perfect illustrations of this are Reno and Las Vegas, Nevada where the police force is three times larger than in cities of comparable size.

No Harmless Pastime

Those who think gambling is a harmless pastime are not facing the facts. As reported in the March/April issue of *Good News* magazine, the Council on Compulsive Gambling of New Jersey has compiled the following shocking statistics:

❖ 68 percent of female gamblers have used illegal means, such as writing bad checks or stealing from employers, to finance their gambling.

❖ Surveys of male and female prisoners in New Jersey, Michigan and Washington, D.C., found that 30 to 40 percent were probably pathological gamblers.

❖ An amazing 13 percent of the prisoners claimed they were in prison because of gambling-related problems.

❖ New Jersey alone has more than 400,000 active compulsive gamblers who affect the lives of 350,000 spouses and 700,000 children.

❖ The attempted suicide rate of the compulsive gambler is 20 times higher than the national average, and the attempted suicide rate of their spouses is 15 times higher.

Gambling Mania

Those who argue in favor of state-run lotteries on the basis that the competition will force illegal gambling operations out of business are often amazed to learn that the reverse is true. After Connecticut introduced a lottery the state's chief attorney, Austin J. McGuigan, observed, "Rather than cut into the revenue of organized crime, that state has been swept by a gambling mania, which has more than doubled the level of illegal wagering in the last eight years."

In Ohio the millions raised for education by the state's lottery provide only a small percentage of the total budget for the state's public schools. Meanwhile voters who think the lottery is "taking care of" education are voting down the local tax levies that provide the backbone of financial support for the school system. Prominent educators argue that the state would be better off without any lottery revenues because it could then find realistic ways to fund its children's schooling.

Gambling is the attempt to get something for nothing. It violates not only the eighth commandment but also the spirit of the whole New Testament because it substitutes chance and fate for the fatherly care of a loving God. I personally believe gambling is a form of stealing.

Many Ways To Steal

But even if we don't steal and don't gamble we should not automatically dismiss the eighth commandment as irrelevant for us. Many unseen values besides property and money can be stolen. Some years ago the president of a great southern university received a letter from a prominent businessman, who was one of the school's most famous graduates. In the letter he enclosed his A.B. degree diploma and wrote "I am no longer keeping something which doesn't really belong to me. I cheated in my senior examinations and did not pass them fairly and squarely. I stole my college education."

Yes, one can steal ideas or answers on an examination. Even the law recognizes that intangible values can be stolen and protects them with copyrights and patents. The state of New York has so many song writers and so many lawsuits over stolen songs that the state hired a specialist known as a "tune detector." This musical lawyer is consulted on these highly technical matters when they go to court.

To cheat is to steal anything, including an honor which is not rightly yours. Stealing is getting the reward without paying the price, collecting the dividend without making the investment. It's receiving money without working, it's making good grades without studying, it's trying for the top of the ladder without climbing the rungs. Like the other commandments, the eighth commandment is written into the nature of God and into the nature of we who are made in his image. Our lives are an investment. Life involves putting something into it and receiving something in return. Stealing, however, is the shortcut philosophy of life that contradicts this basic principle of the universe.

The human desire to take shortcuts formed the basis of Jesus' three greatest temptations in the wilderness (see Matthew 4:1-11). Jesus knew that there could be no crown without a cross, no redemption without the suffering of a redeemer and no resurrection without a crucifixion. But Satan tempted him to get all these without paying the price for them, to steal them. Satan knew people were eagerly looking for a king so he told Jesus to turn the stones into bread, jump off the steeple, put on a display of magic and power, take the shortcut to kingship and get the returns without the investment. But Jesus rejected Satan's suggestions as wrong.

Even God could take no shortcuts when he redeemed us. Jesus was willing to pay the high price. He knocks at the door of your heart, but he doesn't break the lock and burglarize your personality.

Stealing From God

The New Testament also describes another kind of stealing which, from a Christian's standpoint, may be the most serious of all. This is stealing by failing to fulfill our proper stewardship, failing to take what God has given us and use it for God's glory. This is perhaps the highest level of trying to get something for nothing. We steal by accepting something and giving nothing in return. This sin is not doing wrong acts but *failing* to live up to God-given talent and responsibilities. These were the persons in the parables of Jesus who were condemned and punished the most severely.

How do we commit this sin? We can do so in a mate-

rial sense. Malachi 3:8 asks, "Will a man rob God?" It
then explains that we do this when we fail to give him
our tithes and offerings. Now the New Testament takes
us beyond the law of the tenth. The New Testament re-
places the law of one-tenth with the law of ten-tenths.
Everything belongs to God. But if everything belongs to
him in that general overall sense, then the minimum
token and symbol that we must set aside for God certainly must equal that of the law, one-tenth. Are you
stealing from God, keeping for yourself treasure which
is not yours? What some people give to the Lord and to
his church is a disgrace for which someday they will be
held accountable.

We can also steal from God by withholding talents
and gifts from Christ's service, using them selfishly instead. Others who have been blessed with abilities or
material means store and hoard what they have, robbing God of many things which are really his as well as
robbing other people of many blessings.

Our nation claims to have a one-day Thanksgiving,
when we stuff ourselves with turkey and cranberry
sauce. We give our annual nod to God and then forget
him the rest of the year, living as if all the wealth, prosperity and blessings we enjoy belong to us. How can we
do this and expect God's blessing upon our land? This
is robbery on a nationwide scale. Our country of all
countries has taken the Lord's benefits and then forgotten him and turned its back upon his commandments.

We Have Forgotten The Purpose

Our nation, founded upon God's providence and on
Christian principles, prospered in order to be a blessing to the rest of the world. But we have forgotten the
purpose of our nationhood, our destiny among the nations. Remember that the most severe and horrifying of
all of Jesus' parables are those about people who were

given much but who robbed their masters by failing to give them a proper return on their investment (see Matthew 21:33-41, 25:14-30; Luke 16:19-31).

Perhaps the heart of the eighth commandment in the New Testament is found in 1 Corinthians 6:19-20, "Do you not know that your body is a temple of the Holy Spirit. . .? You are not your own; you were bought at a price." The greatest robbery of all is when you and I as Christians take the name of Jesus but fail to surrender ourselves totally, unreservedly and unconditionally to Christ as Lord. Why is this stealing? For the simple reason that when the New Testament says we are to surrender ourselves to Christ, it claims that it is not asking us to give up anything that rightfully belongs to us. It is merely asking us to restore to its rightful owner that which really belongs to him. We are his by creation. We are his by redemption. Therefore, we belong to him.

The eighth commandment says, "You shall not steal." We know we are not to take that which belongs to another. However, do we remember that when we fail to give ourselves fully to him, we are also stealing something that does not belong to us?

11

The Truth About Lying

You shall not give false testimony against your neighbor (Exodus 20:16).

Do not lie to each other, since you have taken off your old self with its practices and have put on the new self, which is being renewed in knowledge in the image of its Creator (Colossians 3:9).

We live in a world full of falsification and lying. Often lying is not even considered a vice, and some people think of it as a virtue or at least an art. Advertisers lie to make money. Politicians lie to get votes. Many people believe that all truth is relative and that nothing is absolutely true or false.

Some say the basic premise of communism, and it could be true of many in high office in our own government, is that if the lies are big enough people will believe them.

One of our greatest problems today is the moral relativism in our courts, which pervades even the dispensing of justice. Clever lawyers twist the truth, confuse even an eyewitness, exalt the false witness and throw so much dust in the air that by the end of the trial no one knows what the truth is. The tragedy of Watergate, for example, was not that we learned the truth but that we will never know the truth.

Against all of this stands the Word of God. This commandment in its original form in the Old Testament probably concerned a simple narrow legal matter of not going to a court of law and lying about a neighbor. But the prophets and later Jesus and the New Testament writers expanded and restated this commandment so that the Bible ultimately forbids every form of lie. There's a reason for this, the same reason we've discovered as the basis for all the other commandments. This commandment is founded on the very character of God himself, and the basic nature of God is truth. It is a vital part of his holiness.

When I taught classes of youngsters preparing for church membership, one of my favorite questions was: "What are some of the things God cannot do?" They immediately responded that God could do anything. I asked, "Can he?" Then we thought a little about the things God cannot do according to the Scriptures. God cannot share his glory, for he alone is God. God cannot violate human freedom, for he gives us the gift of free choice and he will not take it away, even though it cost him suffering on the cross. God cannot tolerate sin. And, of course, God cannot tell a lie.

God is truth. The Son of God said, "I am the way and the truth and the life" (John 14:6). He proclaimed the Paraclete, the coming Holy Spirit, as "the Spirit of truth" (John 14:17). That's why the Bible places the highest premium on truth and truthfulness. Jesus said that one of the basic characteristics of the devil is that "he is a liar and the father of lies" (John 8:44).

Basic Honesty

In 1 Peter 1:16 Peter quotes God from Leviticus 11:44, 45; 19:2; and 20:7 where God says, "Be holy, because I am holy." We could say, "Be truthful, because God is truth." That's why the New Testament emphasizes our attitude towards truth and our basic honesty in life. When God knows our attitude toward a lie, he knows what kind of people we are.

The ninth commandment and its restatement in the New Testament forbid lying in three ways: telling a lie, spreading a lie and living a lie.

First, it forbids telling a lie. Proverbs 6:16 says the Lord hates seven things, and two items on the list that follows are "a lying tongue" and "false witnesses who pour out lies." Revelation 21:8 lists those who will be finally lost, concluding with these words, "and all liars— their place will be in the fiery lake of burning sulphur. This is the second death." Acts 5:1-10 tells the sad and terrifying story of Ananias and Sapphira, who sold their land and told the church and the Apostles that they had given all of the money to the church. In reality they had kept some of the money for themselves. Before their sudden deaths Peter told them, "You have not lied to men but to God."

God's Nature Is Truth

God, whose very nature is truth, who speaks only truth, who loves truth, cannot tolerate our lies. He cannot have fellowship with those of us who tell them. Years ago during a great revival in our church in Bangalore, India, a well-respected leader of the community, under the burning light of the Holy Spirit of truth, wept at the altar with a broken heart. He said, "Oh, I have been such a liar. I have told lies whenever I think it is to my advantage." And some of us here would have to make the same confession.

A lie is a sin against a God of holy truth. Let's be honest about this. Before our conversions some of us were such colossal liars that it took much discipline and a great deal of the Spirit's influence in our hearts to finally establish in us a pattern of telling the truth. Some of us have lied for so long that we really don't know the difference between the truth and a lie. Lying, stretching or manipulating the truth can become second nature to us so that even after conversion we must struggle to break this awful habit.

The Cure For Lying

I only know of one cure for lying. I had to do it in my own life, and it's a horrible remedy. But it's the only cure I know that works: As soon as the Holy Spirit checks you and you catch yourself in a lie, go back and tell the truth to the person to whom you lied.

Some time ago a friend of mine named Dave who lives in a northwestern state was dramatically converted. His conversion shook the sophisticated Methodist church he had been attending because he was the playboy leader of the country club and cocktail set of that church. He was also an exceptionally successful salesman.

A few weeks after his conversion he was closing a sale to the manager of a large company. The manager was on the verge of choosing between two products manufactured by Dave's company. Finally the manager turned to Dave and said, "Dave, tell me which one of these two products company X [a rival company] purchased from you."

Now the difference in the price of the two products, and thus the commission to Dave, was great. Before he realized it, Dave told this company manager a lie, saying that the rival company had purchased the more expensive product from him. Believing Dave, this company manager signed a very large contract for the costlier item.

But the moment Dave packed up his briefcase and walked out that door, he found out he was no longer living alone. The Holy Spirit was living in him. Quick as a flash the Holy Spirit said, "Dave, you told a lie."

And Dave felt miserable. The Spirit said, "You go back and make it right." But Dave couldn't stand the thought of going back to the company manager after making that terrific sale.

This went on for about a day, as long as Dave could take it. The next day he made another appointment with the company manager. After a brief word of testimony, Dave simply said, "My life has been changed by Jesus Christ recently. I've been a colossal liar. I'm sorry, but I lied to you the other day. Please forgive me. The company you asked about bought the cheaper product, not the more expensive one. Now I understand how you must feel about this, so I'm going to cancel this contract. You may not want to do business with a company that would employ a fellow like me. But in case you do, I'll send you another salesman."

Well, as you can imagine, the company manager just sat there with his mouth catching flies. He was speechless. But to make a long story short, he kept the contract and was deeply moved by Dave's testimony.

Now, what Dave did was very difficult, but it cured him—and it will you, too.

"I Can't Stop"

Many people come to me after conversion and say, "I can't stop. I don't know the difference between the truth and a lie." I tell them, "There's only one cure. Every time you lie, go back to the person you lied to and correct it." A college boy once flew into my office a day after his conversion. He said, "Doc, this is killing me."

"What happened?" I asked.

He said, "I wasn't out of your office 20 minutes yesterday till I went to the grill. The guys were all there, and we were bragging. I had been telling all the fellows in the dorm that my folks own a Cadillac, and I said it again yesterday. But just like that, I knew it was wrong, and I had to tell them it was only a Chevrolet. Then last night we were in the dorm in a bull session. We were talking about girls, and I'd told all those fellows for years that I'd been very popular back in high school and had a lot of dates. I started that stuff again, but all of a sudden I remembered I had to tell them that I had been lying. I'd had hardly any dates in high school, and the truth of the matter is, I am scared to death of girls. Doc, it's killing me."

About a month later he came back to my office and said, "Well, it killed me, but it cured me."

Spreading Lies

Second, the Bible condemns spreading a lie as well as telling one. In the long run, sins are measured by their effect on persons. <u>The Ten Commandments are not some theoretical book of rules, but a practical manual on how to get along with other people.</u> The false witness is a sin because it harms a person. Let's face it, this is exactly the kind of lying which otherwise good people are most tempted to do. Scores of the most respectable Christians, who would never dream of murder or adultery or theft, engage in the deadly sin of gossiping and tale-bearing. It's such a pleasant form of sin, isn't it? God takes all the fun out of most sins for us when we are saved. What a pity that isn't true about spreading rumors and malicious tales.

Ironically, we can even feel virtuous and saintly when we commit this sin. We love to talk negatively about others because by putting them down we think we make ourselves look better. But the Bible teaches us that we must be meticulously honest and careful when dealing with the reputation of another person. The devil is the father of these kinds of lies, too—the half-truth, the silent shrug, the quiet nod which gives the impression of agreement, the insidious question, the implication, the insincere praise.

Remember how God praised his servant Job in the Old Testament, calling him "a man who fears God and shuns evil"? But the shrewd devil replied, "Does Job fear God for nothing? . . . You have blessed the work of his hands. . . .But stretch out your hand and strike everything he has, and he will surely curse you to your face" (Job 1:8-11).

Sowing Doubt

When someone praises someone else we, like Satan, say, "Sure. He's good, but look what he's getting out of it. What do you think he's doing it for?" For example, when a person is successful and someone says, "Boy, her career has really taken off," we say, "Yeah, but how do you think she got where she is?" That's all we say. We just sow that doubt.

When a woman is popular and has a lot of dates and someone says, "Guys really like her, don't they?" We agree. Then we deliver the punch line, or rather the line that punches a hole in her character. We say, "Sure, men hang around her. But you know why, don't you?" And that's all it takes.

We need to be scrupulously careful about the damage we can inflict by jumping to conclusions and by spreading our own versions of the truth. That's why James is so afraid of the tongue, calling it "a world of evil" and "a fire" (James 3:6). Proverbs deals extensively with the tongue because it's so deadly, so capable of ruining a reputation, blasting a life and damaging a person's effectiveness.

Once we unloose lies and false suggestions they are impossible to recapture. Children flying kites can haul in their white-winged birds, but we can't recall our words after they have flown. Our thoughts may sometimes fall back dead, but God himself can't kill words after they've been spoken. Have you spread facts you are not sure of, that you later found out were wrong? Then you owe it to your victim to go back to the people you misinformed and straighten it out.

A Living Lie

Third, and this is perhaps the greatest meaning of the ninth commandment, we are not to live a lie. 1 John 1:6 says, "If we claim to have fellowship with him yet walk in the darkness, we lie and do not live by the truth." You see, a lie is something that can be said, spread or lived. One can do a lie as well as speak and spread a lie.

The living lie is the lie of deceiving ourselves. When what we witness to loudly and clearly with our lips is proven false by our life, we are living a lie. The road Jesus took to the cross was lined with this kind of living liar: the scribes who claimed to have knowledge they didn't possess; the Pharisees who claimed to be righteous but were not; the false witnesses who told stories of things they had not seen or heard; Judas, whose loving gesture, a kiss, was the very incarnation of a living lie; and Pilate, who sounded so sincere and pious at the trial when he asked, "What is truth?" to disguise his cowardly, lying heart. You see, the greatest lies of all are the lies we tell ourselves about ourselves. We don't tell these lies for profit or to destroy anyone else but for the sake of our own pride.

The biggest living lie is when we attempt to maintain a false image of ourselves as sinless and not in need of salvation. We try to convince ourselves that this lie is true and to persuade other people that we are something we know we are not. This kind of living lie is described in 1 John 1:5-10. The tragedy is that when we tell this kind of lie to ourselves over and over again we begin to believe it. And then, John says, we are on the dangerous road to destruction.

The greatest challenge I've faced in the counseling room is simply getting people to face the truth about themselves. As the Psalmist writes, "Surely You desire truth in the inner parts; You teach me wisdom in the inmost place" (Psalm 51:6). The Berkeley translation says, "Truth in the inner self."

As a young pastor I soon discovered that most people, including myself, thought my sermons were wonderful truths that were very much needed by someone else. As the prophet wrote, "The heart is deceitful above all things and beyond cure. Who can understand it?" (Jeremiah 17:9). Certainly not you and I.

Modern psychology has actually catalogued many of the deceitful ways we delude ourselves and defend ourselves. We even have a sophisticated psychological phrase for it: defense mechanism. That is a fancy term for living a lie.

Now what hope do we have in all this? Because by nature we're all liars and deceivers, we have only one hope, and that is the Holy Spirit. He is the Spirit of truth. You and I must admit our lies and our deceptions and ask the Holy Spirit to make alive within us the One who said, "I am the truth." When God, the incarnate Son of God, the living truth, lives within us and shows us the truth about ourselves and about God, then we have hope. So let's not end our study of the ninth commandment on the harsh note of the law but on the melodious notes of the gospel.

Facing The Truth

God faced the truth about you a long time ago. Maybe you're just beginning to admit the truth about yourself and find it very disturbing, but God has known it all along. Despite this he has never withdrawn his offer of love. All he wants you to do is to admit the truth.

Our sins don't keep us from God, but our attempts to cover up our sins do.

As we stand before the cross we realize the truth is that we are bad enough to crucify the Son of God. That's the truth about the human heart. God has known that truth a long time, and perhaps now you know it too. Admit it to him. Confess it. The moment you do, the power of the lie, the hold of darkness and untruth, is broken. When we confess and repent of our lies, his Holy Spirit, the Spirit of truth, begins a miracle in our lives, leading us from lying and darkness to truthfulness and light.

12

Are You Master Or Slave Of Your Desires?

You shall not covet your neighbor's house. You shall not covet your neighbor's wife, or his manservant or maidservant, his ox or donkey, or anything that belongs to your neighbor (Exodus 20:17).

What causes fights and quarrels among you? Don't they come from your desires that battle within you? You want something but don't get it. You kill and covet, but you cannot have what you want. You quarrel and fight. You do not have, because you do not ask God. When you ask, you do not receive, because you ask with wrong motives, that you may spend what you get on your pleasures (James 4:1-3).

In some respects the tenth and last commandment is the greatest of the second section of the Ten Commandments. These are the horizontal commandments, those that concern our relationships with other persons. In a sense this final commandment in the Decalogue includes whatever may have been omitted in the others. Nothing like this commandment exists in any other set of ancient laws. It goes beyond regulating outward acts to prescribing inner attitudes. It is certainly the most comprehensive of all the commandments. Perhaps it appears last because the sin it prohibits, covetousness, is the most treacherous of all.

We need victory at this point more than any other. Covetousness makes people greedy and causes them to steal. Covetousness drives people to sacrifice the lives of others, even to kill, for their own ends. Covetousness gives rise to that unbridled lust which plunges individuals into adultery. Covetousness endangers mutual trust and causes people to lie about themselves and each other, to gain money, power, prestige or praise. So the tenth commandment is comprehensive.

What Is Covetousness?

It is also difficult to explain. What does it really mean to covet? Does covet mean to desire something? Certainly not. Without desires we wouldn't have human life as we know it. Our desire for food makes us hungry and we eat. That's how we maintain our bodies. Our desire for sex is an essential part of love and marriage. It leads to the expression of love and to the creation of life itself. We desire approval and respect. That's what makes us wash our faces and comb our hair. Another legitimate desire is to conform to the rules of social etiquette and get along well with others. Without desire we wouldn't have life.

So does coveting mean desiring something that we don't have? Not exactly. For example, many people attend college because they desire an education, something they don't have when they enter college; but this is not coveting. Almost everything we call progress, improvement or civilization has come from a desire for something we don't have. Desire is even important in spiritual matters. Paul says in1 Corinthians 12:31 "... eagerly desire the greater [spiritual] gifts." Jesus also says in Matthew 5:6, "Blessed are those who hunger and thirst for righteousness." No, coveting is not merely a desire for something, even something we don't have.

Buddha, however, taught that desire itself *is* the source of all the evil in the world. He said if we could eliminate all desire we would eliminate evil. Ridding ourselves of desire is supposed to lead us right into Nirvana. That belief has led even some Christians to a false asceticism and a quest for a sort of glorified nothingness. But Jesus did not come to give us nothing; rather he offers us abundant life.

Because of this confusion we have difficulty defining the word "covet," although like a lot of words, we all know what it means. It's kind of like the words "love" and "personality"—they are almost impossible to define but easy to identify when we see them walking down the street.

Desire Run Amuck

To covet is to desire inordinately, or to desire the unlawful. It's not wrong for a man to desire a house, wife, servant animal or car. But it is wrong for him to covet his neighbor's house, wife, servant, animal or car. This kind of desire is different because a desire for someone else's belongings plants the seeds of a willingness to hurt, kill, lie or steal in order to fulfill the desire. Covetousness is desire that runs rampant over the rights of others and even over one's own reason. It is desire run amuck which will injure or destroy to get what it wants. When we feel this type of desire we may even destroy or injure ourselves to get what we want. Covetousness is normal desire gone wrong.

Covetousness is one result of the fall of man. It's a perversion of God-given desires. It's the unbalanced aspect of the human spirit that we call original sin. In this sense coveting is at the heart of the carnal mind. It is the inner principle of sin. "The mind of the flesh" referred to in Scripture is actually a condition of imbalance in our motives and desires. Covetousness is the defect in our internal power-steering mechanism that pulls us toward the wrong. It's the spirit that says, "I want this and I will get it whatever it costs me. I must have it, whatever the consequences."

A practical substitute for the word "covet" might be "greed," provided we understand this can mean more than simply greed for money. We can be greedy for power, sex, approval, authority, praise, status and so forth. Covetousness is hard to define, but we know it when we see it.

Universal Problem

Let's examine the universality of covetousness. Another good reason for this commandment being last is because it's such a universal sin. Covetousness is the last enemy of both the sinner and the saint.

Almost every language and culture has proverbs about covetousness. In English we say, "The grass is always greener on the other side of the fence." One of Aesop's fables tells how a man killed a goose that laid golden eggs, concluding with this moral: "Much wants more and loses all." A Scottish proverb says, "The covetous man will never have enough until his mouth is filled with mold." In India a Hindu proverb says, "If you mention money, even the corpse opens its mouth."

Covetousness affects every level of human life. We find it in the church, in ourselves, in our own community. Christ taught sacrifice and selflessness, yet we see little of that in our lives. Even godly ministers have fallen prey to covetousness by desiring prestige and authority in the church.

The spirit of covetousness has broken every system of government ever devised by mankind. Although it threatens our Democratic system, our nation has survived many crises because our founding fathers invented a system of government that recognizes the

universality of covetousness. Universal human selfish-
ness and covetousness wrecks every theory of utopia,
every dream for peace and prosperity from More's
utopia to Marx's communism. Man will covet. It's a universal sin.

David And A Little Lamb

Nathan the prophet realized this (see 2 Samuel 12:1-
13). The Lord sent Nathan to King David after David
had committed adultery with Bathsheba and murdered
Uriah, her husband. However, Nathan didn't talk to
David about murder or adultery. Instead, he told the
king a story about a rich man who had a big ranch with
lots of sheep and cattle. One day an important friend
came to visit and the rancher wanted to throw a party.
But he didn't go out to his ranch and kill one of his own
sheep for the feast. Instead he turned to a poor man in
the community who had only one little ewe lamb, a
family pet. The rich man could have chosen from a vast
herd, but he took the only lamb the poor man owned.
Covetousness, Nathan the prophet pointed out, was
David's sin.

Anyone who has reared children knows how early in
a child's life covetousness emerges. When we lived in
India I remember giving my son Steve a good, expensive knife. It was something he wanted and needed
there, and he was happy as a lark with the gift. Then
one day he came into the house crying. "What's wrong,
Steve?" I asked. Tearfully he told me his playmate had
been given a knife with two blades on it. Covetousness
is a mirage that produces wretchedness because it fixes
our gaze on something we do not have so that we don't
praise God for what we *do* have.

Greed is idolatry, Paul writes in Colossians 3:5. God
created our hearts to be satisfied only by fellowship
with him. Anything less will not truly satisfy us. Cove-

tousness is idolatry because it places a substitute for
God in our hearts. Therefore, the tenth commandment
brings us back to the first commandment because covetousness puts a false god in the place of the true God in
our lives. Greed seeks first the kingdom of things, not
the kingdom of God.

Even our religion can become a form of covetousness. We try to use God to get what we want. If you don't
believe that, listen to the self-centeredness of some of
our prayers.

Because of the universality and the treachery of the
sin of covetousness, this commandment is different
from every other commandment in the Decalogue. All
the others deal with specific actions: "Don't do this," or
"Do that." Only this tenth commandment forbids a state
of mind and heart. This tenth commandment was the
little spark of light that one day Jesus would make perfect in the full revelation of the New Testament. That
light was the realization that wrong ideas and wrong
desires precede wrong actions. No matter how pious our
outer life may be, if we yield inwardly to covetousness,
we are guilty of breaking the commandment.

This Old Testament commandment, although stated
as law, is really the forerunner of grace because it deals
with the attitude not just an act. It goes to the heart.

In the Old Testament this commandment is only
stated negatively. It forbids us to covet anything, but it
doesn't tell us how to stop coveting. It doesn't tell us how
to cure this terrible disease. It doesn't tell us how to stop
being slaves and how to become masters of our desires.

Balancing The Heart

However, Jesus made this commandment positive
as well as negative. He taught that the cure for covetousness, the way to change this great imbalance in the
human heart, is to let the Holy Spirit restore our hearts

to their intended balance. That happens only when we completely surrender ourselves to the lordship of Jesus Christ. Only when we seek first the kingdom of God and his righteousness will other things be given to us (see Luke 12:31). To accomplish this change we need a new birth, a conversion, a change of outlook and a change of values. Since covetousness is a sin of the inner life, our supreme need is to be set right within our hearts.

Paul, for example, surrendered himself to Christ—his ambition; his education; his great ability as a speaker, a writer and a leader; and his philosophical mind. What did he say after this surrender? "I have learned to be content whatever the circumstances," he writes in Philippians 4:11. Was Paul content with his spiritual progress? Oh, no. He also writes in Philippians 3:14, "I press on toward the goal to win the prize for which God has called me heavenward in Christ Jesus." Was Paul content with the world around him? Oh, no. He longed for people to know Jesus Christ as Savior so deeply that he likened the desire to the pains of childbirth (Galatians 4:19). He was not content with his spiritual progress or the world around him. Paul had a divine discontent. Then what *was* he content with? He was content with the direction of his life, with the will of God as he found it in Jesus Christ. He was satisfied with Jesus. Today that's still the only cure for covetousness.

A New Master

Are you a slave to your desires? Or are you the master of your desires? The only way to change, to become a master, is to be mastered by Jesus Christ. We must find a new master who brings contentment so that we too can say, "For to me, to live is Christ and to die is gain" (Philippians 1:21). The only answer to covetousness, this basic characteristic of the mind of the flesh, is a total surrender to God and a total infilling and cleansing of his Holy Spirit. "Rejoice in the Lord always. I will say it again: Rejoice!" writes Paul (Philippians 4:4). Phillips renders this verse, "Find your delight in God." That's the answer to covetousness. Find your delight in God, surrender your will, power, success money and recognition to Christ. Be his slave, his love slave as Paul often called himself. This cure for covetousness is described in 1 Timothy 6:6 as: "godliness with contentment." The New Testament positively affirms "You shall not covet" by teaching us to be content in Jesus Christ.

Dr. W.E. Sangster tells a wonderful story about the saintly John Fletcher. He and the other early Methodists were anything but far-out pietists. Their holiness included helping everybody in the community, sacrificially giving to the poor, visiting people in prison, even riding on those horrible carts with men from the infamous Newgate prison who were going to the gallows to be hanged for petty crimes.

A Gift The Mayor Couldn't Give

John Fletcher did so much to help his community that he was brought to the mayor's attention. Some officials decided that since Fletcher wasn't well-off financially the government ought to give him a gift. So someone from the government called on Fletcher and gave him a few pounds in an envelope. But when John Fletcher saw what it was he gave it back to the visitor. The gentleman took the money back to the mayor, who said, "Well, I guess we didn't give him enough." So they increased the gift by a few pounds, but again Fletcher refused the gift. The mayor said, "Well, maybe he wants more," so for the third time the gentlemen took the gift to Fletcher. But John Fletcher returned it again, saying, "You don't understand. I don't want it."

"Well," said the exasperated mayor's representative, "you must want something. We want to show our appreciation. What can we give you?"

Fletcher said, "No. Honestly, there's nothing I . . . well, there is one thing I want."

The man got out his notebook, ready to write the request. Fletcher said, "I only want more grace."

13

The Law And The Gospel: Opposing Forces?

But now, by dying to what once bound us, we have been released from the law so that we serve in the new way of the Spirit, and not in the old way of the written code (Romans 7:6).

In many ways this is one of the most important chapters in our study of the Ten Commandments. It is also the most difficult. The relationship between the law and the gospel is not easy to understand. People wonder, "What is the role of the law of God and the commandments of God in the life of the Christian?"

If we say we are saved by faith alone, then where does the law fit into the picture? If we say that we cannot be saved by keeping the law, then how can one be lost by breaking it? Does the true Christian live above the law in a sense, as "he is not under law but under grace" (Romans 6:14)? Just what is the relationship between the law and faith, the commandments of God and the gospel?

Answers to these and related questions do not come easily. Through the centuries equally scholarly and saintly Christians have answered these questions in a variety of ways.

I think it is helpful to examine two of the most extreme answers. Both have been based on Scripture and experience taken out of context. As we examine these two opposites, somehow we find the great paradoxical truth the Scripture uses to relate law and grace.

Extreme Law, Extreme Grace

It's a historical fact that one extreme breeds another extreme. Although the two ideas we will explore are poles apart, they actually produce and sustain each other. Perhaps by avoiding the extremes we can find a balance and can discover the truth.

One extreme holds that for all practical purposes, the law or commandments do not exist in the Christian life. However, people who believe this do not understand the difference between the law and legalism. Because Jesus tangled with the Pharisees and criticized their legalism, they assume that Jesus opposed any kind of law or commandment. Because Paul strongly opposed the Jewish legalistic custom of circumcision insisted on by the early church's so-called Jerusalem party, and stressed salvation by faith alone, these people reason that Paul too viewed no law as binding upon Christians.

People who think this way come from every spectrum of theology. Some have a very liberal Christian background. The most famous of these are people like Joseph Fletcher, who wrote the book *Situational Ethics*, or John Robinson of England, who wrote *Honest to God* and many other books. John Robinson didn't invent the phrase, "the new morality," but he popularized it. These men in essence say that there is no law except the law of love, no absolute except love. Their liberal tradition emphasizes the new morality, and we have dealt with many of their arguments earlier in this book.

But many evangelicals within the church believe this way too. For instance, several years ago the leadership of a certain well-known evangelical youth organization crumbled because of this issue. An insider told me how, for example, if a meeting were announced for 9 a.m. some staff members would drift in at 9:30 or 10 or 10:30. When the supervisor would reprimand them they would reply, "We're not under law, we're under grace." We may laugh at this absurd behavior, but a host of similar incidents actually split a great organization.

I know my source was telling me the truth about this group because one night I invited some of them to visit the church I pastored in Wilmore, Kentucky. It was springtime, and I was preaching one of my annual sermons about the sanctity of sex to my congregation, which contained many college students. The sermon was titled something like, "Why wait 'til marriage?" and highlighted the biblical injunction against fornication. Afterwards members of this visiting group took me to task in my office. They told me I was preaching legalism and putting false ideas in young people's heads. They noted that Paul said that to state the law always provokes and incites sin, and indeed Paul does say something like that (see Romans 7:8), but they had taken it out of context.

Now this "lawless" version of Christianity couldn't be further from the truth, whether it emerges from a liberal or evangelical camp. We must be careful not to misinterpret Jesus' run-ins with the Pharisees or some of Paul's statements about the law as biblical proof for this position.

"You Have Heard It Said. . . ."

In the Sermon on the Mount (Matthew 5-7) Jesus six times introduces his teachings on Christian conduct by saying, "You have heard that it was said. . . , but I

tell you." However, Jesus in no way contradicts biblical
commandments because he is not referring to the "it
was written," but the "it was said," which was a technical interpretation of God's law. The Pharisees had invented these elaborate interpretations, thus turning
God's commands into their own legal code. Jesus,
however, restated the original Old Testament commandments and made them much tougher. As we've
seen in previous chapters, he applied them not merely
to external action but to internal attitudes, making the
commandments stricter and harder to follow.

Paul writes in Romans 13:8-10, ". . .he who loves his
fellow man has fulfilled the law. The commandments,
'Do not commit adultery,' 'Do not murder,' 'Do not steal,'
'Do not covet' and whatever other commandment there
may be, are summed up in this one rule: 'Love your
neighbor as yourself.' Love does no harm to its neighbor. Therefore love is the fulfillment of the law." Here
Paul goes out of his way to restate five of the six horizontal commandments, those dealing with relations between humans. Paul does not say that they are to be
discarded but that they are to be kept as an expression
of love for one's neighbor.

Interdependence Of Love And Law

Love and law are not incompatible or mutually ex-
clusive. Love needs law to guide it. It is naive to say that
love doesn't need anything outside of itself, as though
it has a built-in moral compass which enables it to zoom
in on the right action. Love is not infallible. It is sometimes very blind and stupid. So God has given us commandments, guidelines that tell us how love should
behave in order to be loving towards one's neighbor.

John Stott explains this beautifully in his portion of
the book *Christ the Controversialist*: "Love is not the finish of the law in the sense that it dispenses with the

law. Love is the fulfillment of the law in the sense that it obeys it. What the New Testament says about law and love is not, 'if you love you can break the law' but rather 'if you love you will keep the law.'"

What about Paul's statement to the Christian, "You are not under law but under grace"? He says this several times in various ways. To truly comprehend this we must remember that the Bible never suspends its negatives in thin air; they're always in context and usually in contrast to something. In every passage where Paul says that we are not under law but under grace, he simply means that no Christian depends on the law as the means of his or her salvation. Paul does not mean that God's commandments are abolished for the Christian but that the Christian does not look to the law for justification or sanctification. In other words, Paul is saying this: "Your efforts to live a good life according to God's commandments cannot save you. Only faith in God's grace can save you; only the Holy Spirit can sanctify you. No law can do it."

Evidence Of Salvation

But just because Paul says the law is no longer the basis of our salvation, he does not mean that we should dispense with the law. In fact he says exactly the opposite. He says in effect, "Now the Holy Spirit himself will write God's laws on your hearts and help you to live by them" (see Romans 5:5, Galatians 4:6-7 and Hebrews 8:10). The Holy Spirit will not only help you live by them but also live by them joyously and lovingly. Indeed, says Paul, this new way of living, of obedience to God's command, is one of the evidences that you have received salvation (see Romans 5:17, Ephesians 4:22-24 and Colossians 3:9-10).

The Bible never says, "Love God and do what you please." Over and over again it gives us commandments and principles which shape our love for God and other people. The Bible answers the 64-dollar question that always has to be asked at some point in the Christian life: "What kind of conduct does love require of me?" As we've seen, the Bible answers that question both negatively and positively.

The negative answers are important because they fence off an area where we are free to learn what love means. The "thou shalt nots" of the Scripture mark the edge of the road of love that we are to travel. Jesus is blunt about this. In Mark 7:20-23, Jesus lists 13 major sins in no uncertain terms. Paul, in Galatians 5:19-21, gives another list, flatly saying, "I warn you, as I did before, that those who live like this will not inherit the kingdom of God." The greatest love chapter in the Scriptures, 1 Corinthians 13, describes only seven positive attributes of love but lists nine negatives ("love does not" or "love is not"). Scripture plainly teaches that love is the fulfillment, not the abolishment, of the law. Some absolutes cannot ever be made relative. And yet many Christians fall into this trap.

'I'm Saved; I Can Do Anything'

I was surprised during an interview several years ago with high school youth that so many of their questions concerned the role of God's law in the Christian life. One said, "I have a good Christian friend who says 'I am saved, so I can do anything. I don't have any laws.' What do you say about my friend?" My answer was that the friend is not saved but self-deceived. 1 John 1 says in no uncertain terms that we deceive ourselves and the truth is not in us if we say we have fellowship with the One who is light, yet continue to walk in darkness.

Some of us need to genuinely repent of genuine sins in our lives. We need to pray with the Psalmist for a clean heart and a new spirit and for God to restore the joy of salvation (see Psalm 51:10,12). I have spent hours counseling people who have torn down all the moral fences and are now wandering in a miserable wasteland. God in his love has given us the law as a guideline for loving contact.

But now let's discuss the opposite extreme. Some people err in the other direction, ending up with a Christian life that is a strange mixture of law and grace, faith and works. This approach borders on legalism.

In the Bible the best examples of this viewpoint are the Pharisees and the so-called Jerusalem party or Circumcision Party in the early church. The word "Pharisee" means "separated ones." These religious leaders were called that because they withdrew from the Sadducee Court about 150 years before the time of Christ. The Pharisees were determined to resist the increasing influence of Greek culture. They decided that the only way to do this was to separate themselves from everyone else and to maintain certain man-made traditions and interpretations of the Jewish law. By the time Jesus arrived, the Pharisees had a list of 248 dos and 365 don'ts, one don't for every day of the year. And they meticulously observed all their rules. That's why Paul, who was formerly a Pharisee, could honestly say in Philippians 3:6: ". . .as for legalistic righteousness, [I was] faultless."

More Don'ts Than Dos

Even today some Christians pride themselves on their separatedness. They have chosen the Pharisees' strategy for fighting the tides of change. These people have taken a list of man-made laws, called them convictions and given them the status of absolutes. For all practical purposes, among most Christians this list of standards is what distinguishes them from nonChristians. Like the Pharisees, those of us who think this way

usually have a lot more don'ts than dos. Most of those
don'ts represent human opinions on amoral issues
which have evolved during the last 50 to 100 years. A
lot of these rules concern matters of appearance and
other trivial matters.

A letter written in the second century A.D. sounds
startlingly modern. A young man writes to a celebrated
Christian, one of the church fathers: "Sir, I am in
earnest about forsaking the world and following Christ.
But I am puzzled about worldly things. What must I for-
sake?" The celebrated Christian answers in a letter,
"Colored clothes, for one thing. Get rid of everything in
your wardrobe that is not white. Stop sleeping on soft
pillows. Sell your musical instruments and don't eat
any more white bread. You cannot, if you are sincere
about obeying Christ, take any more warm baths or
shave your beard. To shave is to lie against him who
created us, to attempt to improve on his work."

We could fill an entire book with lists of things that
were once considered deeply sinful that we now take for
granted, not only as a part of daily life but even as a
vital part of Christian life and worship. For example,
many of our churches contain pipe organs but not many
years ago thunderous sermons were preached denounc-
ing that horrible instrument of the devil.

Someone once asked me an interesting question.
"You know," this person said, "we've noticed that you
missionaries and ex-missionaries seem to give your
children a lot more freedom. We thought you would be
strict parents, yet you seem to have much more relaxed
standards than other Christians. Why?"

Culture And Opinion

I had never thought about this, but I believe the
questioner was right. It only takes a few months on a
mission field to discover that about half of the impor-

tant rules in our evangelical circles are purely matters of American culture and opinion and have little or nothing to do with the essentials of the gospel or even God's basic commandments.

Perhaps every missionary has had an experience something like Elisabeth Elliot's. I certainly did when I went to India as a missionary. Elisabeth Elliot in her book *The Liberty of Obedience* tells how after her husband was martyred she returned to live for several years among the very Indians who had killed him. She writes about her struggle in trying to communicate the gospel to those people. Her problem was that she tried to teach them all the dos and don'ts she had learned in the United States. She says in effect that, after the end of the first week, she ran out of sins to preach about because these people didn't have the slightest interest in anything she'd denounced. This does not mean that our standards are not important, but they are *not* the heart of the gospel. They're cultural American accretions, barnacles on the good ship Zion.

Contradictory Behavior?

Now, those who insist that we are not really Christians if we don't follow certain dos and don'ts are doing the opposite of what Paul taught about standards for non-absolute matters. Paul taught that in some circumstances you ought not to do something, but in another set of circumstances you *should* do that very same thing. In one situation he'd eat meat without any question of conscience, but in another he wouldn't touch it (see 1 Corinthians 8). In one case he would recommend circumcision, but in another he would literally die before he would do so (1 Corinthians 7:8-9 and Galatians 5:2-6). Is there a principle behind such seemingly contradictory behavior? Yes. We cannot make relatives absolute any more than we can make absolutes relative.

Relatives are constantly changing and need updating and rethinking under the direction of the Holy Spirit. This is the kind of mature Christian conscience that Paul says he is in travail to produce in his converts (see Galatians 4:19 and Colossians 2:6-23).

Relatives And Absolutes

I want you to understand what I am saying. I have no time for the extremes of the new morality or an evangelical doctrine which permits a sinning Christianity. No such thing exists in the New Testament. No intellectually honest student of the Bible can conclude from the phrase, "We're not under law but under grace" that ours is a sinning religion.

But I also see the serious damage that's done when we equate human standards with absolutes. Too often this causes us to confuse God's absolute, unchanging, eternal standards with our relative, human beliefs. Unfortunately people who confuse the two tend to throw them both out together. This is a tragedy which I see happen all the time. We must understand the difference between God's eternal commandments, which never change, and relative standards which, by God's grace and direction of the Holy Spirit, we are obligated to change as our times change.

So what guidelines do we live by? Do we misunderstand Paul like the imaginary opponent he argues with in Romans 6:1 and 6:15: "What shall we say, then? Shall we go on sinning so that grace may increase? . . . Shall we sin because we are not under the law but under grace?" Paul answers both rhetorical questions with an emotional Greek idiom that has been translated as "God forbid!" "Perish the thought!" or "Under no circumstances!" Without the law we do not become lawless. As we read Paul's epistles we find that he takes the middle of the road. He does not make the tragic error that so many are committing today by following the extremes of the old moralism or the new morality.

After Paul explains that the law is not a means of achieving salvation, he immediately explains the real purpose for which the law was given. The law is a guideline for our conduct, to tell us how love behaves and how to obey God in order to please him. It contains ethical principles to teach us *how* to love God and to love our neighbor as ourselves. The law is no longer an external instrument of justification or sanctification, a code we must try to follow. The law for the Christian is internal as the blessed Holy Spirit writes those laws upon our hearts and empowers us to keep them. "You, my brothers, were called to freedom," writes Paul in Galatians 5:13-14, "But do not use your freedom to indulge the sinful nature; rather serve one another in love. The entire law is summed up in a single command: 'Love your neighbor as yourself.'"

A Christian Badge

Some time ago a woman asked me about a certain recently converted young person. "How is he getting along?" she inquired.

"Oh, fine," I said. "I think he is really growing in grace."

"Well, I don't seem to see the evidences of that growth in grace," she said.

"What do you mean?" I asked.

She recited a long list of external matters, mostly related to appearance, in which she thought the new Christian was still lacking. I didn't say anything and she continued, "You see, those things are like a badge a person wears. Every Christian wears a badge, an identification mark. When I don't see those things in this young person's life, it is as though he is not wearing the right badge, so I do not identify him as a Christian."

Now her reasoning and her spirit were good. The problem was that she was looking for the wrong badge. Jesus said that Christians do wear a badge, and he defined it for us. If we wear this badge it will help us avoid the extremes we've discussed by bringing the law and gospel together in the proper balance. In John 13:35 Jesus says, "All men will know that you are my disciples if you love one another."

14

Reflections On The God Who Gave The Commandments

And God spoke all these words, saying, "I am the Lord your God, who brought you out of the land of Egypt, out of the house of bondage (Exodus 20:1-2).

Having explored the nitty-gritty of the commandments themselves we still must do something very important. No study of the commandments is complete without reflecting on the One who spoke the Ten Commandments.

Listen to the first commandment: "You shall have no other gods before me." Who receives the command? You— a second person personal pronoun. Who gives the command? I do—a first person personal pronoun. Most people interpret those personal pronouns as "it." They read the commandments as though an impersonal "it" is forbidden to do such and such by another it in an impersonal law book. But there are no "its" there. The commandments contain an "I," first person, God, and a second person, "you."

You see, the Ten Commandments are words spoken by a person, God, to a world of persons. They are guidelines for the personal relationship between God and us and between us and other human beings.

That's why John writes that all who keep *his* commandments, not *the* commandments, will abide in him (1 John 3:24). Or conversely, "The man who says, 'I know him' but does not do what he commands is a liar, and the truth is not in him" (1 John 2:4). The basis of Christian morality is very simple. If you want to know what is good and right or what is bad and wrong, you look to God. The character of God determines what is good. His commandments express his character and his nature and tell us what his will is for us as persons. Therefore the Christian standard for all goodness is personal, based on the personality of God himself. So to understand the Ten Commandments we must understand God's uniqueness and character.

We are treading some rather deep theological waters here. Let's fast-forward from Exodus to a particularly difficult aspect of the Christian understanding of the nature of God: the Trinity. Although at first glance it may seem unrelated, this doctrine is essential to our understanding of the commandments; especially to the idea that the greatest commandment of all is to love God and each other.

Christians say there is only one God. The first commandment says, "You shall have no other gods before me." But then we claim that God is three-in-one, a Trinity. When we say that we face a tremendous mystery.

The Trinity Mystery

The story is told that the great thinker, St. Augustine, was walking along the seashore one day while pondering the Christian doctrine of the Trinity. He seemed to hear a voice saying, "Pick up one of the large sea shells there by the shore." So he picked it up. Then the voice said, "Now pour the ocean into the shell." And he said, "Lord, I can't do that." And the voice answered, "Of course not. In the same way, how can your small, finite mind ever hold and understand the mystery of the eternal, infinite, triune God?"

The logical mathematician tells us that one plus one plus one equals three. But the singing, worshiping, adoring heart of the Christian replies, one times one times one equals one. Here's another example. A mother has three sons and writes each a letter saying, "Son, I love you with all my heart." Now, logically, that's impossible. But every parent knows what she means. The mathematically impossible can be true when it comes to love. The Trinity is not such a problem for our hearts as it is for our heads.

But we're not just hearts and emotions or heads and reason. We can't separate one from the other. We've got to try to understand the Trinity. The Ten Commandments are based on the character of God and the essential quality of God is his triune nature: God the Father, the Son and the Holy Spirit.

Clever Theologians or Simple Teacher?

People make two great mistakes regarding the Trinity. Some think the Trinity was invented by clever theologians. Certainly theologians exist, but they didn't appear until after the early church was well established. The other mistake occurs when folks take the opposite approach and say, "Jesus was a simple teacher from Galilee. We're complicating the gospel by talking about the Trinity. Let's just stick to the simple gospel and the teachings of Jesus." The trouble is that people who talk that way are picking and choosing only the parts of the New Testament that they can easily comprehend and dismissing the rest. They do not confront the real mystery of our faith.

How did the idea of Trinity get started? The early Christians experienced the Trinity long before they ever thought about a theology of the Trinity. What they experienced was so new and revolutionary that it broke all of their old intellectual molds.

Remember, the earliest disciples were all Jews. They had been trained from their childhood to say, "The Lord thy God is one God and thou shalt have no other gods before me." They were fierce monotheists.

A Man Like No Other

But Jesus was a man like no other man. He lived sinlessly before them. He performed miracles before their eyes. He gave them incredible truths and insights which he said he received directly from God. He claimed a previous existence with God, his Father. He dared to forgive sins. He said he was going to die and give his life to atone for the sins of the entire world. He did die on a cross. He was buried. He came back from the dead. He walked and talked with those disciples for 40 days. He left them saying, "I'm leaving, but in a sense I'm coming back. My other self is going to come, the Holy Spirit. It will be as though I am still with you, only this time He's going to be in you." Then Jesus rose into heaven.

Now what could the disciples do? They knew what kind of a person Jesus was. Did they abandon the God of their past, the Creator of the world, Jehovah? No. Did they simply add Jesus to their religion as another god, giving them two gods instead of one? No. The apostles realized this was a mystery. They didn't understand it, but they couldn't deny it. They were forced to conclude that the Father in heaven is God and that Jesus of Nazareth, Christ, is God. God actually incarnated himself in the human life of Jesus of Nazareth.

But that was not the end. The early Christians had another experience. True to the risen Christ's word, the Holy Spirit came at Pentecost. The disciples were invaded by a Presence and a Power so absolutely real that they looked at each other and said, "So this is what Jesus promised! He said he was coming back and that he'd live in us." The disciples became new persons. They were literally taken over by another person, the very life of God himself. Was this Holy Spirit a third God? No. It was the same God of creation, the Jehovah of the Old Testament, who came to live with us in Christ.

No Obtuse Doctrine

So you can see that the disciples did not get together to concoct some obtuse doctrine about God being three persons. First, they experienced this three-personal God so powerfully that they were forced to conclude, against all their monotheistic beliefs, that God must include Father, Son and Holy Spirit. After they had experienced God in this mysterious way they remembered that Jesus told them to go into all the world and baptize in the name of the Father, the Son and the Holy Spirit. Then they remembered the Old Testament words from Genesis 1:26 where God says, "Let us [plural] make man in our [plural] image." The early Christians began to put it all together. The experience of the Trinity came first; the theology came later.

Christians believe in the Trinity because nothing less than God in three persons adequately explains God's nature and our nature, which form the basis of the commandment to love. That sounds complicated, so let me explain.

One of the most amazing modern discoveries or rediscoveries is that giving and receiving love is essential for human existence to reach its full potential. It's a scientific fact that love is the key to life. Sociologists tell us this from the standpoint of society and the community. Biology and medicine have proven that love and loving relationships are necessary for the physical growth of a little baby. Research shows that a baby can be fed, clothed and kept warm and comfortable, but if it isn't given love it may die. Love is crucial to human existence—physically, emotionally, spiritually.

Made For Love

Psychologists and psychiatrists say this in a thousand different ways. From a baby's first days through every stage of human life, we have to have love. We're made for love. We can't be healthy without it.

My point is this: all the sciences, from their own viewpoints, are saying something very biblical. They're saying that love is not just some sentimental feeling. Love is not a luxury option added on to life. Love is vital for the proper functioning of a human being. Christians have always said it. But today secular non-Christians, agnostics, even atheists are saying it in no uncertain terms.

But why is this true? Does this need for love have a basis in the creation, in the very structure of life? At this point Christians have an advantage over the rest of the world. We who believe in the Trinity can shout triumphantly, yes! Love is not just a biological product resulting from the interaction of glands and chemicals and hormones. Love is not just a social pattern that man has learned through millennia of trial and error.

We Christians can know that God in three persons, our God, is a social God. God in the very structure of his life is God of love. Love is an echo in human time of the voice of eternity. Our human experiences of love—the bond of love between two friends, the flame of love binding a man and a woman together, the unfathomable love of a mother for her baby, the sacrificial love of a patriot for his or her country, love in every shape and form—do not exist by chance. They exist because love is fundamental to the nature of God himself. God is love.

But how long has God been love? Since he had crea-
tures to love? Since he had beings who could love him
in return? No. Because he is eternal and everlasting, he
always was, always is and always shall be love. Before
the first particle of stardust in the universe, before the
first animal, before the first human being, God was love.

The Christian doctrine of the Trinity means that the
one eternal and divine life of God has three centers of
consciousness and will. Bound together with perfect
love are the Father, Son and Holy Spirit. They exist in
perfect harmony, perfect love, perfect oneness of
thought, feeling and decision. The life of God is perfect
eternal unselfishness. The Father exists in and through
the Son. The Father loves to glorify the Son. The Son
exists through the Father. They all exist in each other
and in the Holy Spirit. Each one's joy is to glorify the
other. Jesus says his glory and joy is to glorify the
Father. Jesus also told the disciples that the Holy Spirit
would come not to glorify himself but to glorify Christ.

Selfless Love

God is not an eternally lonely person existing in
splendid isolation amid his own perfection, loving himself but commanding you and I to love unselfishly. This
would mean God asks us to do something that he has
not done. We would be unlike God rather than like him
when we love, which would destroy the whole basis of
the Christian life and the commands to love. Instead
the doctrine of the Trinity tells us that selfless love is
grounded in the character of God himself.

This sounds awfully theoretical, maybe even far-
fetched. But remember that in John 17:11 Jesus prays,
"Holy Father, protect them [the disciples]...so that they
may be one as we are one." God doesn't command us to
do anything that he doesn't do.

But what does this have to do with the Ten Commandments? The answer is "everything." All the commandments are fulfilled, as Jesus taught us, in the great commandments to love God with all our hearts and to love our neighbor as ourselves (see Matthew 22:37-40). Why? Because God is perfect love. That kind of a God has a right to command you and me to love.

We believe in the Trinity because it explains the New Testament Christians' experiences of God and answers our own deepest needs. But more than that, it gives us the key to life and all of our relationships. Jesus says in John 13:34, "A new commandment I give you: Love one another. As I have loved you, so you must love one another."